Praise for *Beyond Quick Fixes*

"This useful and well-written book doesn't pretend to be a substitute for psychotherapy, but it offers valuable insights and suggestions that not only complement and enhance what one learns in therapy, but can contribute to a richer and fuller life in their own right. It doesn't talk down to the reader or oversimplify, but in clear and vivid language provides an authoritative guide to accessing our full selves based on state-of-the-art theory and research."

—**Paul Wachtel, PhD,** CUNY Distinguished Professor, City College of New York, author of *Making Room for the Disavowed* and *Therapeutic Communication*

"In a world increasingly drawn to shortcuts and superficial remedies, *Beyond Quick Fixes* offers a refreshing and much-needed alternative. Dr. Birkhofer invites readers to cultivate the deeper inner resources that truly sustain well-being. This important and timely contribution reminds us to patiently develop the capacities that enable us to live with greater awareness, resilience, and purpose."

—**Tal Ben-Shahar, PhD,** author of *New York Times* best seller *Happier*

"Blending clinical wisdom with deep compassion, this book illuminates how our minds shape our lives—and how we can change them. A clear, empowering guide for anyone seeking greater insight, resilience, and emotional freedom."

—**Shauna Shapiro, PhD,** best-selling author of *Good Morning, I Love You: Mindfulness and Self-Compassion Practices to Rewire Your Brain for Calm, Clarity, and Joy*

"A wonderful synthesis of wisdom, drawing from a rich tapestry of trustworthy sources. This book invites you on a journey to discover and reclaim your unique sense of individuality and personal authenticity. A process of deep self-reflection and learning empowers you to work with your mind, emotions, values, and 'inner warrior' as catalysts for personal growth."

—**Margaret Black, LCSW,** psychoanalyst and coauthor of *Beyond Freud: A History of Modern Psychoanalytic Thought*

"Dr. Birkhofer offers hope, encouragement, and guidance for anyone wanting to improve their mental health and fortify their inner resources. This valuable roadmap—including compelling personal stories, experiences with patients, clear explanations of the science of the mind, and self-assessment tools—empowers you to build upon your strengths and modify behaviors and mindsets that can interfere with your ability to thrive and make positive changes."

—**Denise Pope, PhD,** Senior Lecturer, Stanford University; Co-founder, Challenge Success; author of award-winning book *Doing School: How We Are Creating a Generation of Stressed-out, Materialistic, and Miseducated Students*

"Weaving together lessons from personal experience and patient stories, Dr. Birkhofer adeptly explores the human 'internal operating system,' that often runs on autopilot. She guides readers through a powerful process of self-reflection and inner work, arguing that while meaningful change can be challenging, the investment in yourself is well worth the rewards."

—**Laura Erickson-Schroth, MD,** chief medical officer for the Jed Foundation (youth mental health and suicide prevention)

"A beautifully written text, rich with valuable insights, information, and guidance. Dr. Birkhofer draws wisdom from over four decades of clinical work and personal experience, and the result is inspired and compelling. Whether or not you are directly struggling with mental health concerns, every reader who aspires to a more meaningful life will benefit from the lessons, exercises, and thoughts shared in this work."

—**Laura Roberts, MD, MA,** Professor and Chair, Department of Psychiatry and Behavioral Sciences, Stanford University School of Medicine

"Written with clarity, wisdom, and care, this rich and compassionate roadmap—informed by Dr. Birkhofer's own personal journey with suffering and loss—explores the essential qualities of mental, emotional, and relational well-being. Exercises, examples, and reflective tools help readers loosen the grip of old patterns of being, relating, and coping to cultivate new experience, healthier behaviors, and a more deeply connected life."

—**Harville Hendrix, PhD,** and **Helen LaKelly Hunt, PhD,** authors of the *New York Times* best seller *Getting the Love You Want*

"Dr. Birkhofer masterfully consolidates a lifetime of experience and wisdom into a compassionate roadmap for understanding the mind, healing, and personal growth. Her insights empower you to become a more authentic, fulfilled, and capable version of yourself. This is a truly meaningful contribution to people's well-being!"

—**Scott Barry Kaufman, PhD,** best-selling author of *Transcend: The New Science of Self-Actualization*

"Beautifully written . . . full of wisdom. Dr. Birkhofer cuts through the noise and guides you back to center—to what truly matters: your own internal operating system that needs care and attention to operate with greater courage, authenticity, serenity, and wisdom. The world needs this wake-up manual now. What a gift!"

—**Stephanie Brown, PhD,** author of *Speed: Facing Our Addiction to Fast and Faster—Overcoming Our Fear of Slowing Down*

"*Beyond Quick Fixes* turns away from simple solutions toward the slower, braver work of personal growth. With warmth and clinical wisdom, Dr. Birkhofer offers readers practical guidance for strengthening resilience, relationships, and wiser action in the face of pain. A thoughtful, compassionate guide to lasting change."

—**Steven C. Hayes, PhD,** Foundation Professor Emeritus of Psychology, University of Nevada Reno, author of best sellers *A Liberated Mind* and *Get Out of Your Mind and Into Your Life*

Beyond Quick Fixes

Beyond Quick Fixes

ESSENTIAL INGREDIENTS *for* BETTER MENTAL HEALTH *and a* FULFILLING LIFE

Dr. Celeste Birkhofer

GREENLEAF
BOOK GROUP PRESS

This book is intended for informational and educational purposes only. It is sold with the understanding that the publisher and author are not engaged in rendering psychological, medical, or other professional services. The material presented is designed to encourage self-discovery and personal growth, but it is not a substitute for professional mental health treatment, diagnosis, or advice.

If you suspect you have a condition requiring professional intervention, please seek the assistance of a qualified healthcare provider. To protect the privacy of individuals, all patient stories have been modified. Names, identifying characteristics, and factual details have been altered, and some examples are composites of multiple individuals. Consequently, any resemblance to actual persons, living or deceased, is purely coincidental.

Published by Greenleaf Book Group Press
Austin, Texas
www.gbgpress.com

Distributed by Greenleaf Book Group

For ordering information or special discounts for bulk purchases, please contact Greenleaf Book Group at PO Box 91869, Austin, TX 78709, 512.891.6100.

Design and composition by Greenleaf Book Group
Cover design by Greenleaf Book Group
Cover image used under license from ©Unsplash.com

Publisher's Cataloging-in-Publication data is available.

Print ISBN: 979-8-88645-525-0

eBook ISBN: 979-8-88645-526-7

To offset the number of trees consumed in the printing of our books, Greenleaf donates a portion of the proceeds from each printing to the Arbor Day Foundation. Greenleaf Book Group has replaced over 50,000 trees since 2007.

Printed in the United States of America on acid-free paper

26 27 28 29 30 10 9 8 7 6 5 4 3 2 1

First Edition

For my son, Wiley—

Your love and spirit live on in all who knew you.

Contents

INTRODUCTION: Take Care of Your Mental Health 1

1: Defining Good Mental Health, Fulfillment, Happiness, and the Essential Ingredients 9

2: An Introduction to the Mind and Development 19

3: Your Sense of Self and Its Parts 33

4: A Healthy Sense of Self 47

5: Mental Capacities 65

6: Emotional Capacities 81

7: Relational Capacities 99

8: Healthy Coping Strategies 123

9: Your Journey of Personal Growth and Development 145

APPENDIX A: Resources

Recommended Reading by Topic 167

APPENDIX B: Exercises

The Caring Behaviors Exercise 171

Identifying Your Strengths and Positive Qualities 175

Values Clarification Exercise 179

Questions to Understand Your Development 187

Self-Assessment: Your Essential Inner Resources 193

APPENDIX C: Additional Mental Health Resources 207

ACKNOWLEDGMENTS 209

NOTES 213

BIBLIOGRAPHY 223

INDEX 231

ABOUT THE AUTHOR 241

INTRODUCTION

Take Care of Your Mental Health

"What lies behind us and what lies before us are tiny matters compared to what lies within us."

—Ralph Waldo Emerson

From the outside, I looked like a thriving, well-adjusted college student, but under the surface, depressive feelings engulfed me, often at the most inopportune times. My relationship to food and exercise was far from healthy. Bingeing on Stan's Donuts or ice cream before running five miles to burn off the calories and guilt made it clear that something wasn't right, but I didn't understand why, or how to rid myself of the compulsion. I had little capacity to tolerate uncomfortable thoughts or feelings, so I avoided them. I stuffed them down with food or stayed busy. I didn't know how to be in touch with or communicate my needs and desires, so I suppressed them and focused instead on pleasing others. I had no idea what "authenticity" meant, so I shaped myself into what others expected or thought I should be, pursuing what the world said was admirable and appropriate. My intrinsic desires seemed irrelevant. I was unaware that my difficulties and approach to life had been so significantly shaped by the ways I learned to adapt to my experiences growing up, some of which were no longer serving me well.

My father, a good man and colonel in the army, struggled with alcoholism and depression, something our family never talked about openly. My mother did her best to raise seven children, and I tried hard not to be a burden to her. I often felt alone and overwhelmed by confusion, sadness, and fear. My father eventually sought help, though it was long after I'd learned to cope by suppressing my needs and emotions and being overly accommodating, driven, and self-reliant.

With the help of a therapist, I began a process of developing myself from the inside out—strengthening aspects of my inner world that were underdeveloped and learning healthier coping mechanisms. Healing and personal growth changed my life in profound ways and sparked a lifelong interest in psychology. I set out to learn all I could about the causes of psychic pain and difficulties navigating life, as well as how people heal and change. I earned graduate degrees in Marriage and Family Therapy, Clinical Psychology, and Contemporary Psychoanalysis. Helping people understand themselves and improve their lives has been immensely rewarding. Then, in 2014, a tragic, life-altering event further deepened my passion for encouraging others to improve and take better care of their mental health to the best of their abilities.

My son Wiley was diagnosed with bipolar II disorder during his freshman year at Stanford University. Wiley was an incredibly bright, creative, and loving human being. After fighting a courageous and exhausting nine-year battle with mental health problems, he sadly died by suicide at age 27. It seemed as if a deteriorative process invaded his mind and slowly robbed us of what had once been our full-of-life son. It was utterly heartbreaking, gut-wrenching, to witness how the illness that hijacked his mind seemed to keep one step ahead of all the efforts he made to get well. That devastating loss was a frightening reminder of what's at stake, of how critical mental health is to everything else that matters in life, including life itself.

The quality of our mental health impacts every aspect of our lives: our moods, thoughts, attitudes, feelings, actions, and choices. Global research says that the quality of your mental health is the single most important factor explaining the difference in people's happiness.[1] Improving your mental health matters. You matter. And it is worth the effort.

Mental Health Challenges and Hopeful Remedies

So many people are struggling to function well, feel good about themselves, and create fulfilling lives. Approximately 25 percent of adults in the United States experience a mental health disorder every year, and half the population will face one by the time they reach age 75.[2,3,4] Millions of people are suffering from depression, anxiety, or a painful sense of disconnection. An alarming number of people die from suicide and drug overdoses every day. Globally, only 33 percent of adults rate their quality of life high enough to be "thriving,"[5] and only 44 percent of Americans say they are "very satisfied" with the way things are going in their personal lives.[6]

Poor mental health can have devastating consequences, impacting individuals and society in profound ways. Living with untreated mental health conditions increases the risk of physical health problems, addiction, substance abuse, homelessness, and suicidality. It puts a strain on interpersonal relationships and frequently interferes with work, school, and other activities, contributing to job loss or poor performance, academic failures, and financial instability. Beyond statistics, poor mental health causes tremendous suffering.

Most people long to be mentally healthy, happy, and fulfilled. Unfortunately, many of us are lacking useful knowledge and are under-resourced or misguided in our approach to realizing those desires. In pursuit of happiness or pain relief, we're often seduced by quick fixes that rarely produce meaningful change: social media "likes," addictive substances or activities, or overly simplistic three-step plans for self-improvement. We often look outside ourselves to feel better—more possessions, status, or fleeting highs—and in the process, *we ignore what's most important.*

What matters is tending to the internal operating system that dictates the quality of our lives, something that takes time and effort to understand and reprogram. If your car isn't running well because the engine needs a thorough inspection and proper repairs, a new paint job isn't the right remedy. Similar to upgrading the software on your computer, you need to understand what operating system is running your mind so you can work on upgrading it to the best version possible.

As a society, we're drowning in information and starved of wisdom. The booming self-help industry signals a collective hunger to bridge the gap between where many of us are and where we want to be. But it's challenging to find trustworthy resources that provide useful direction for realizing personal transformation. This book fills that gap and teaches you the essential ingredients that make a significant difference. Feeling good about yourself and your life, coping with complex problems, meeting your needs, healing, evolving, and creating longer lasting fulfillment all deserve—and require—more attention and effort than quick fixes provide. We need to invest our time and energy in what is most likely to have lasting value and truly impact the quality of our mental health and lives. Meaningful transformation and improvements in our mental health come from developing a foundation of reliable internal resources and qualities that make us more capable of functioning well, living fully, and coping effectively.

What to Expect on This Journey

In over 40 years dedicated to understanding the complexities of the human mind and assisting people on their journeys, I've witnessed firsthand the remarkable transformation possible when you invest in personal growth and inner work. In this book I've synthesized and distilled decades of academic scholarship and clinical insights about good mental health, optimal functioning, and human fulfillment into an actionable framework for developing inner resources and psychological capacities—from connection and curiosity to resilience and emotional intelligence—that can unlock your most capable, authentic self.

You deserve a valuable, potentially life-changing, comprehensive roadmap for understanding what factors shaped and influence your mental health, and for navigating the intricate landscape of your mind. This book offers more than superficial tactics. It transcends the allure of simplistic or short-lived solutions and offers a wealth of information and guidance that goes beyond providing advice on a singular aspect of your mental health to provide an all-inclusive overview of what you need to create a stronger foundation for good mental health. True personal transformation is not a one-size-fits-all or one-simple-fix endeavor, but it does include a similar assignment for all of us: Understand your own mind and psychology and develop inner strengths and capabilities.

While this book doesn't attempt to address all the challenges and complexities related to more serious mental illness, it's a valuable resource for most people—those who want to be better informed, recover from difficult past experiences and various mental health problems, recognize and modify ways of being that no longer serve them well, and improve their overall well-being and mental health.

Everyone should have easy access to useful information and resources that can help them in this process. The book includes patient stories, writing exercises, and self-assessments to help you understand yourself, identify your strengths, and determine what still needs further development so you can create and embark on an individualized plan for personal growth and improved mental health.

Life introduces an ongoing stream of both highs and lows. While most of us enjoy the good times, we seem to have greater difficulty navigating the harder parts of being human—the disappointments and challenges. Yet all human experience includes difficulties, uncertainty, loss, and pain. While we cannot control all of what life throws our way, we have some agency over who we are, how we evolve, and how we respond to the hands we are dealt—even when the outcomes are not quite what we wanted or had envisioned. If we prioritize taking good care of our mental health, we can develop the capacities to understand the complexities of our mind and emotions, modify our less healthy ways of being and relating, develop better coping strategies, and become more positive agents in our lives. We can discover and learn to access dimensions of ourselves that can help us live more authentic and fulfilling lives.

Few things hold more sway over the quality of our lives than our mental health. I encourage you to embrace continued personal growth for meaningful change. The journey, while demanding, can enrich your life. In a world increasingly challenged by psychological suffering, the need to prioritize your mental health and make a greater investment in what lies within could not be more essential and timely.

It's hard to think of anything more valuable than becoming someone wise and self-aware who can regulate emotions, form strong relationships, cope with challenges, and have a healthy sense of self. Someone, in other words, equipped with the essential ingredients that lead to a strong foundation for better mental health, who can successfully navigate life in all its complexity and live fully and meaningfully. Let's get started!

CHAPTER 1

Defining Good Mental Health, Fulfillment, Happiness, and the Essential Ingredients

"Happiness is a by-product of a life well lived."

—Eleanor Roosevelt

Before we dive into the heart of the book—teaching you the inner resources to develop within yourself for better mental health—let's define some terms to broaden your understanding of how all these topics are related. As it turns out, many of the same internal qualities and capacities that lead to good mental health also contribute to greater fulfillment and longer lasting happiness.

This chapter answers the following questions:

- How is good mental health defined and what does it include?
- What does research say about creating a fulfilling life?
- What is the difference between happiness and fulfillment?
- What essential ingredients help us create better mental health and fulfillment?

Defining Good Mental Health

Let's start by clearing up two misconceptions about good mental health:

Myth #1

Mental health is simply the absence of mental illness.

Myth #2

People with good mental health are always happy.

> Good mental health is the integration of important internal capacities with ever-evolving capabilities that enable you to function effectively in life.

Humanistic scholars such as Carl Rogers and Abraham Maslow viewed good mental health as the presence of positive states of human capacities and functioning in thinking, feeling, and behaving.[1] The U.S. Surgeon General defined mental health as: "A state of successful performance of mental function, resulting in productive activities, fulfilling relationships with people, and the ability to adapt to change and to cope with adversity."[2] Both definitions of good mental health highlight the importance of functioning well in multiple areas. Having good mental health means you possess the essential resources that enable you to create a satisfying life and cope effectively.

The *Psychodynamic Diagnostic Manual* (PDM-2) outlines categories of basic mental functioning that are critical components of good mental health.[3] Impairment in any of these areas of functioning impacts your mental health. Examples include

COGNITIVE AND AFFECTIVE PROCESSES

- Be able to experience, understand, and communicate the full range of emotions
- Regulate your attention, emotions, and thought processes
- Reflect on and learn from your experiences

SELF-AWARENESS AND SELF-DIRECTION

- Be aware of and be informed by your different states of mind, and those of others
- Operate with a degree of self-confidence and agency
- Construct internal standards and values to guide you, and find meaning and purpose

IDENTITY AND RELATIONSHIPS

- Maintain a realistic representation of yourself and others
- Develop self-esteem that is not unrealistically high or low
- Engage in healthy interpersonal relatedness and mutually satisfying relationships

DEFENSES AND COPING

- Modulate impulses and express them in an adaptive manner, and tolerate frustrations
- Cope effectively with challenges, and grow and learn from setbacks
- Cope in ways that do not overly distort reality or create negative consequences

HOW COMMON IS GOOD MENTAL HEALTH?

Research estimates that 50 percent of adults have "moderate mental health," 20 percent of the adult population meets criteria for "flourishing," 10 percent of the population is "languishing," defined as an absence of mental health but not currently dealing with a mental illness, and 20 percent of adults are actively experiencing a mental health disorder.[4,5,6]

Flourishing adults are characterized by positive self-acceptance, emotional well-being, purpose and satisfaction with life, positive psychological and social functioning, and a commitment to personal growth. They report the fewest mental and physical health problems and the highest levels of psychosocial functioning, self-reported resilience, and intimacy. When compared to flourishing individuals, moderately mentally healthy and languishing adults exhibit greater impairment in both the physical and mental domains. Languishing and moderate mental health are associated with greater limitations of daily living, more reduction of work productivity, more chronic physical disease, and poorer psychosocial functioning.[7]

Mental illness episodes tend to increase when a person's overall mental health decreases.[8] And, mental illness episodes that occur in someone who is already languishing (lacking good mental health) are more debilitating than episodes occurring in someone with a baseline of moderate or good mental health. That said, even individuals with good mental health can have episodes of mental illness.

As stated earlier, half of all adults will experience at least one episode of mental illness before they turn 75,[9] and every year, approximately 25 percent of adults will experience a mental illness.[10] It's not uncommon to struggle with your mental health at some point in time to varying degrees, and it's nothing to feel ashamed of. Bigger problems arise when you ignore your suffering, don't seek help when needed, or don't make any effort to develop inner resources as a protective factor. You're less likely to have mental health problems, and you're more able to recover from them if you actively address issues as they arise and fortify your inner resources.

While it's important to continue offering quality treatment to those who suffer from mental illnesses, it's equally important to educate people on how to develop and maintain good mental health. Currently, our culture puts more focus and resources into treating illnesses than preventing them, but medical leaders are beginning to consider the limitations of a healthcare system that is primarily *reactive* to illness and crises.[11]

Many studies show cost-saving benefits associated with preventative care.[12, 13] The time is right to shift attention toward what we can do to develop better mental health and fortify ourselves with inner resources that help us not only survive but also give us our best shot at flourishing.

What Do "Happiness" and "Fulfillment" Really Mean?

If you ask people what they want most in life, or what they want for their children, they often say, "I want to be happy," or "I just want my children to be happy." It makes sense that most of us want to be happy, successful, and free from pain and mental health disturbances. Understandably, we tend to prefer less sorrow and more joy.

But life is not that simple. Life is often rather complicated. Most of us don't really understand all that's involved in creating a life that works well—what optimizes good mental health, awakens joy, keeps us from languishing, allows us to thrive and create good relationships, and provides meaning and fulfillment.

While I won't delve too much into philosophical or spiritual musings about the meaning of life, happiness, and fulfillment, I hope this brief overview of some of the research will illuminate the connection between good mental health, fulfillment, and the essential ingredients and inner resources this book will expand upon, further motivating you to invest in your personal growth and development.

THE DIFFERENCE BETWEEN HAPPINESS AND FULFILLMENT

Researchers study two kinds of happiness:

Hedonic happiness is associated with the pursuit of pleasure, good feelings, immediate gratification, positive feelings derived in the moment, and the avoidance of pain. Examples of hedonic happiness include enjoying tasty food, getting attention, getting high on substances, and the thrill of winning a game. These feelings tend to be short lived.

Eudaimonic happiness is derived from living a life of purpose, meaning, authenticity, and personal growth. It's more about the lasting satisfaction that comes from living up to one's potential, acting in accordance with your values, and making a contribution to something larger than yourself.[14]

Both kinds of happiness have places in our lives, but if you choose to rely primarily on hedonic happiness, chasing momentary highs, then you are likely to be disappointed. Hedonic happiness can lead to compulsively chasing one thing after the next—anything that makes you feel instantly happy.[15] When you do, you get a hit of dopamine, the neurotransmitter that activates your brain's pleasure center. But the dopamine high doesn't last, and you can become vulnerable to developing addictions, as you increasingly need to have more and more of "the thing" to feel any pleasure at all or avoid withdrawal symptoms that can come from not engaging in the addictive behavior.[16] If you pursue eudaimonic fulfillment, on the other hand, you're likely to lead a happier life over the long term.

Research shows individuals who report higher levels of self-acceptance, purpose in life, positive relations with others, autonomy, mastery, and personal growth generally report being happier and more satisfied in their lives.[17] The founder of positive psychology, Dr. Martin Seligman, conducted extensive research into what contributes to well-being, flourishing, and a fulfilling life. He identified five critical elements:

- **Positive emotion:** feelings of satisfaction, serenity, joy, optimism, and contentment
- **Engagement:** being fully absorbed and focused on tasks of importance to you
- **Good relationships:** participating in satisfying social connections

- **Meaning:** serving something bigger than yourself
- **Accomplishment:** developing mastery in certain areas

Other research identifies personal growth, authenticity, and finding purpose as three main sources of fulfillment.[18] Living a life that is deeply suited to you and feels worthwhile comes from developing yourself, being true to your authentic self, realizing your potential, and making a positive difference in the lives of others.

While hedonic happiness is about feeling good—and we certainly need and want to savor moments of bliss, joy, and awe—eudaimonic happiness is centered on the satisfaction with living authentically, with purpose, and being able to function well. While research acknowledges that both types of happiness matter, high levels of eudaimonic well-being typically lead to greater *sustained* happiness and life satisfaction.[19] This research provides additional incentive to develop the five inner resources laid out in this book, as they will help you not only function better but also create greater fulfillment and eudaimonic happiness.

Defining Essential Ingredients and Inner Resources

Essential ingredients that help us create a foundation of better mental health and a fulfilling life include: being curious and informed about our own mind and tendencies; a willingness to invest in the development of the five important inner resources that enable us to function well; and the wise use of external support and resources.

The five inner resources were derived by combining characteristics of good mental health and optimal functioning with the contributing factors for eudaimonic happiness and fulfillment. They are briefly introduced in the following list, and an entire chapter will be devoted to helping you understand and assess your current strengths with each of these important capacities.

ESSENTIAL INNER RESOURCES:

1. **A Healthy Sense of Self** includes self-worth, authenticity, using your personal agency and values to create a fulfilling and meaningful life, self-awareness, and self-compassion.
2. **Mental Capacities** include the ability to self-reflect, be mindfully aware, gain insight, focus your attention, plan and strategize, and use good judgment.
3. **Emotional Capacities** include the ability to recognize and tolerate your emotional experiences, learn from and process feelings, and regulate them using self-soothing, deeper understanding, and constructive thinking and action—all resulting in greater emotional intelligence.
4. **Relational Capacities** include the ability to form and maintain healthy and mutually satisfying relationships, using self-awareness, personal growth, mutual recognition, and effective communication skills.
5. **Healthy Coping Strategies** include the ability to effectively cope with challenges, protect yourself in healthy ways, and build resilience using self-awareness, acceptance, compassion, good attitudes, and constructive action.

A deeper understanding of yourself and a willingness to invest in your ongoing development, along with wise effort and action, will help you become the kind of person who can successfully navigate life's highs and lows. You can become someone who is aware, insightful, can regulate emotions, form good relationships, effectively cope with life challenges, and have a healthy sense of self.[20]

Before we learn more about that process, the next step is learning how our minds work and how we develop, which lays the groundwork for understanding your own psychology and internal operating system, ultimately giving you greater agency over modifying sources of suffering or limitation that are negatively impacting your life.

CHAPTER 2

An Introduction to the Mind and Development

"The mind is a subjectively perceived, functional entity that governs the total organism and its interaction with its environment."

—Dan Siegel

The mind creates internal mental models of what we have learned through experience, and those models have an ongoing influence on how we behave and view ourselves, others, relationships, and the world. The mind emerges from the activity of the brain, and its structure and function are shaped and influenced by biology, our experience with others, and our environments. It is created within the interaction of internal neuro-physiological processes and interpersonal experiences. The mind includes conscious and unconscious beliefs and attitudes, thoughts, emotions, a sense of self, and ways of being.[1]

Our mind essentially acts as our operating system. It deals with a constant barrage of input and is tasked with managing our numerous and sometimes conflicting needs, desires, feelings, and concerns. Our minds process thousands of thoughts and hundreds of emotions a day to make sense of our experiences and direct our decisions and actions. We contend with 27 different categories of emotions, which are natural and spontaneous responses to our moment-to-moment experiences in life.[2] Emotions tend to evoke pleasure (e.g., happy, satisfied, peaceful), unpleasantness (e.g., mad, sad, disgusted), or fear (e.g., anxiety). Needless to say, there's a lot going on in there.

The Mind's Efficiency

For efficiency's sake, the mind is divided into conscious and unconscious memory. Cognitive consciousness, or working memory, includes awareness. It's a limited resource, so it must be used sparingly.

Procedural memory (remembering how to do things like ride a bike, drive a car, and relate to others) and emotional memory operate largely on the unconscious level. Believe it or not, roughly 80–95 percent of behavior is executed unconsciously.[3] The mind consolidates many of our ways of being and coping strategies into long-term memory, allowing them to operate automatically.

> In essence, we run on autopilot most of the time.

While efficient from a cognitive standpoint, this operating system can prove problematic when our autopilot mode includes counterproductive thoughts and habits that interfere with creating healthy and satisfying lives. This is true for almost everyone. Most of us learned at least a few coping strategies growing up that enabled us to survive or adapt to less-than-ideal conditions, but eventually, some of those strategies cause other problems.

There's no such thing as a perfect childhood or developmental environment. Caregivers are fallible, imperfect beings, and things can and do go wrong with our biology. Certain sociocultural influences, including social media, can also prove to be harmful. Unfortunately, no one's autopilot comes pre-installed with all the important psychological capacities we need to have good mental health; they must be developed. Your autopilot simply reflects what you have learned, experienced, and internalized thus far—helpful and unhelpful. Fortunately, it can be modified.

Autopilot can also be explained in biological terms: Neural pathways are created in the brain that represent repeated patterns of behavior, thought, and feeling that become associated or paired. The more they repeatedly occur together, the stronger the associated neural pathways become. When these neural pathways get activated by certain stimuli or triggers, they direct our behaviors, operating out of conscious awareness.

Many of our habitual coping mechanisms are examples of pathways that have been established for years. For example, you may have learned to suppress your sadness or anger by eating, which now shows up as food cravings when you're sad or angry, even when you aren't physically hungry. Those emotions and that behavior got paired in your neural circuitry. You may reach for cigarettes or alcohol when you feel anxious or stressed to reduce sensations of tension and anxiety. Or you might bite your nails to soothe anxiety or distract you from that emotion.

Scientists say, neurons that fire together, wire together, and when certain stimuli and behaviors get wired together in your brain, they become automatic responses and habits. To change the habits, then, you need to weaken undesirable neural pathways and create healthier neural pairings. Thankfully, with conscious effort and practice you can learn to respond to certain situations or feelings (stimuli) with greater curiosity, encouragement, compassion, tolerance for your feelings, healthy self-soothing, and strategic thinking. This allows these healthier responses to get paired up with certain stimuli, creating new wiring to compete with old, less helpful wired-in responses. Our brain's capacity to change throughout our lives is called "neuroplasticity."

Your mind is a fascinating, complex adaptive system, the development of which is influenced by interacting forces from your biology, as well as sociocultural and interpersonal environments. Through the accumulation of our experiences, the mind develops beliefs about who we are, what we can expect from our environments, how relationships and the world work, and many autopilot tendencies and ways of being. You end up with an "operating system" that can and does run largely on autopilot, and this book will help you become more aware of what your autopilot tendencies are so you will be more capable of modifying them.

How We Become Who We Are

One of our most important developmental tasks is learning to get our needs met, and our mental health is significantly impacted by how well or poorly that process unfolds.[4,5,6,7]

Our primary human needs include

- **Physiological needs:** We all have certain biological needs—food, shelter, basic safety, sensual and sexual needs—that need to be met.
- **Personal needs:** We need to feel valued and recognized (to feel like "I matter"), and to have a sense of agency or influence over our lives, to protect and assert ourselves, play, explore, and create. A higher-level personal need is to self-actualize or live up to our potential.
- **Relational needs:** We're born with strong innate drives to form connections and attachments. We need to feel a sense of belonging and experience intimacy—to give and receive love.
- **Existential, transcendent, or spiritual needs:** We need to find meaning and purpose in life, to be guided by values that matter. The need to transcend goes beyond self-actualization as it connects us with something greater than ourselves, allowing us to make a contribution to others and the world.[8]

We start out in life entirely dependent upon our caregivers for food, comfort, safety, and connection. Whether and how our needs are met contributes to the development of unconscious expectations regarding safety, trust, and love. We develop beliefs about who we are, what we can expect from our environment, and how relationships and the world works. If we were lucky, we had caretakers who were responsive, caring, wise, and encouraging. We grew up having our basic needs adequately met, and we felt valued, loved, and seen. We developed a healthy sense of self rooted in basic self-worth.

When our caregivers are responsive to our needs and help us deal with challenges, we develop important psychological capacities through a process of internalization. Our experiences become part of who we are. For instance, if our parents soothed us when we were hurt or afraid, we eventually develop the capacity to soothe ourselves. If a caregiver helps us think through challenges and goals, we internalize the capacity to reflect on our experiences, make sense of them, and plan and make good decisions. If we are encouraged to express and explore our desires and opinions, we develop agency, which enables us to play an active role in shaping our experiences.

If we were appropriately supported, but not overly rescued or shielded from challenges, we learn to face difficulties and develop resilience. If we were able to repair ruptures in our relationship with our caregivers, we develop trust and more secure attachments. The healthy experiences we had with others become internalized and develop into capacities of our very own—a process of co-creating the inner resources and capacities we need to function well in life.

Unfortunately, the process of getting your needs met and developing important inner resources and psychological capacities isn't simple and doesn't always go well. Sometimes our environments aren't adequately responsive, and we're forced to make the best of what's available, using unsophisticated or barely effective methods for just getting by. Children quickly learn what their caregivers can handle or provide, and they adapt to the conditions they're born into. Caregivers may have competing needs of their own or challenges, limitations, or stressors that make it difficult for them to adequately respond to their children's needs.

Exposure to childhood trauma negatively impacts development and roughly 60 percent of adults in the United States report at least one type of adverse childhood experience before the age of 18.[9] Abuse and neglect, along with family difficulties stemming from stressors such as addictions, violence, mental illnesses, and poverty, intensify other risk factors, such as genetic or biological susceptibility to emotional and cognitive difficulties, as well as lack of resources and support.

Chronic exposure to trauma can alter brain structures that we need to function well, including the prefrontal cortex, which is responsible for executive functions like decision-making, planning, and impulse control. It can also lead to an overactive amygdala, the part of the brain responsible for the "fight or flight" stress response, resulting in heightened emotional reactivity and increased anxiety.[10] Childhood trauma often leads to the creation of more desperate survival strategies that don't typically serve us so well later in life.

If you experienced trauma or had other significant challenges as a child, such as physiological impairments, you should be compassionate and patient with yourself. Your development was derailed by influences outside of your control. There will be work to do to heal from your traumas and improve your abilities to navigate difficulties and protect yourself in healthier ways.

> Becoming who you are, and your continued evolution, is a complex process—embrace your unique history and journey and get support.

My patient Sophia (whom we'll discuss more in the next section) experienced terrible neglect, as she was left to fend for herself as a child. Sophia adapted by trying to suppress or ignore her needs, becoming invisible to her parents, and she eventually became invisible even to herself. Another patient, Mia, was verbally and physically abused, and she adapted by fighting back, using anger and aggressive measures to protect herself and get some needs met (you'll hear more about her story in another chapter). These different forms of coping helped them each survive difficult aspects of their childhoods and became part of their autopilots. As adults, they each had to relearn many things, including what it means to care for and love oneself, and develop better ways to address their needs, cope, and relate to others.

Most of us enter adulthood with aspects of our personalities, habits, and autopilot tendencies that could use some attention. Once we're adults, we must take responsibility for our personal growth and development, doing what we can on our own, and making use of other trustworthy people who can help co-create important capacities within us.

> We all have room to grow more fully into the best versions of ourselves.

Change, or the resumption of development, is facilitated by understanding what your unconscious tendencies, expectations, and beliefs are, where they came from, and the purpose they served. Once they're brought into the light of awareness, they can be learned from and altered. A deeper understanding of your autopilot—appreciating how you came to be the person you are, combined with sufficient opportunities for new and better experiences—can help you heal and keep evolving. My patient Sophia is an example of what's possible.

SOPHIA'S STORY

Sophia was raised by a mother who struggled with chronic depression and a father who worked long hours and seemed distant and irritable most of the time. She painfully recalls him exclaiming, "I never wanted children in the first place!" and her parents sometimes referred to her as "the accident." She felt unwelcome in her own home and experienced herself as a burden. Her parents didn't tolerate noise in the house, so Sophia learned to suppress not only her needs but also other expressions of exuberance or curiosity, fearing they would evoke irritation or anger. Although full of questions about herself, others, and life, she slowly but surely shut down her inquisitiveness, making herself quiet, small, and unimposing.

In high school, undiagnosed dyslexia left her feeling stupid. Her shame was compounded by a period of promiscuous behavior, as sexual encounters became one of the few ways she felt noticed and desired. Deep down she craved being seen, wanted, and touched. She was called a "slut" and the label was hard to shake. Her peers seemed to enjoy being judgmental and cruel, ranging from indifferent to gratified by the pain and suffering they ignited. She felt unworthy at home and at school.

Sophia's developing sense of self and her expectations of others were colored by her experiences of neglect, rejection, and shame.

She disavowed parts of herself that didn't feel welcome, such as her excitement, interests, needs, and feelings. She increasingly adapted to her circumstances by ignoring needs that she sensed were bothersome to others. At times she despised her needs: What was the point if they either irritated others or couldn't be met? She assumed her authentic, more expressive self was simply "too much" and learned to expect very little from the people in her life. She became resigned to beliefs that she had little value or potential and shouldn't hope for something better.

Fortunately, Sophia had one friend and one teacher who were kind to her and showed some interest. They kept a flicker of hope alive in her—maybe some people could care about her or see something of value in her. Maybe she did matter and was worth other people's time and attention.

Sophia came to therapy seeking help for an eating disorder and depression. She felt empty inside. Food provided a temporary comfort, something within her control, and it helped keep feelings and needs stuffed down. Initially, Sophia needed a lot of help acknowledging her emotions. She often changed the subject when feelings emerged, so I slowed her down and sat patiently with her while she learned to tolerate and explore her emotions. Grief and disappointment were the most recurring ones at first—sadness over how little she knew about or loved herself, how shut down she had become, and grief over what she missed out on growing up. She also learned to accept conflicting feelings, such as moments when she excitedly started trying new things and simultaneously felt terrified.

"Starvation" was another vague but deep feeling we began to explore, an emotional hunger. Sophia had become so detached from her needs over the years that it took a lot of guessing at first to get in touch with what she was most hungry for. It took some convincing that it would be worth the pain of "opening this can of worms," as we called it, to be aware of how much she was missing in her life, to see how hungry she was for connection with others, recognition, freedom to express herself, affirmation, comfort after a hard day, and for a break from the relentless studying she was doing at community college to prove she wasn't "stupid."

Next to Sophia's "can of worms" was an old storage trunk with a lock and note on it saying, "DO NOT OPEN." It contained most of her repressed, unprocessed feelings. She wasn't yet aware of the freedom and healing that would emerge from opening that trunk, how important it would be to have someone bear witness to and validate all she had endured and held by herself for so long. Gradually, she began to open up.

Sophia shared how difficult it was having a mother who could hardly get out of bed in the mornings, held hostage in some mysterious and debilitating dark hole. She woke up each morning to an eerie emptiness after her dad went off to work early; made herself a baggie full of dry cereal to eat while walking to school; arrived home with no one to greet her with a hug, a snack, or curiosity about her day; went to bed at night with no one to tuck her in or read her a story when she was young. It was relieving and healing for her to let the flow of messy tears run down her face, and to have someone respond with tenderness and compassion. Her feelings and experience were no longer confined and isolated in the locked-up trunk.

Very slowly, Sophia found the courage to experiment with new ways to meet her needs. She discovered she liked hot baths, long walks, and novels. She worked on her troublesome relationship to food and eventually learned to mindfully enjoy eating again, rather than keeping herself on strict diets only to later binge with reckless abandon. She joined the school theatre club and began asking classmates to hang out, hoping to make new friends.

As she began to understand how her childhood had shaped her views of herself and the world, the void she felt and her pain and struggles started to make more sense. Eventually, Sophia's mom sought treatment for depression, and the two began repairing their relationship. Sophia found the courage to talk to her mother about how agonizing it was to feel like her mere existence was unpleasant for her parents. She came to realize that she wasn't unworthy of love but that her parents both had their own serious difficulties that made it hard for them to be responsive. Her mom was eventually able to show some love and interest after she received treatment for depression.

Over time, we nurtured back to life parts of Sophia she'd disavowed, like enthusiasm, silliness, and curiosity. Sophia came out of hiding and found ways to once again want and work for things that mattered. She challenged beliefs that were harming her, such as believing that she was a burden, unlovable, incapable, or permanently tainted by her past behavior. She had more compassion for the unsophisticated strategies she'd used to cope when she was younger, understanding that was the best she could do at the time. Under better conditions and with enough time and psychological safety, Sophia gained important insights into herself. She expanded her capacities to think, feel, and relate to others in ways that enriched her life. She regained access to a fuller version of herself, someone she grew to accept, love, and believe in.

When you understand the complex factors that have influenced your development—biological, psychological, and sociocultural—you can hold those insights with compassion and appreciate how you became the person you are. Then you can begin to question some of the unhelpful or faulty assumptions you learned to make about yourself, others, and the world.

> Who you became as a result of your childhood is not all of who you can be.

You can modify your autopilot using insights and new experiences. There is no expiration date on growth and personal development. It is a lifelong journey.

Development Is an Ongoing Process

Good mental health and a fulfilling life can't be bought. At some point after childhood, we all have the opportunity to consider what kind of inner work could improve the quality of our mental health and lives. We need to take responsibility for modifying tendencies that contribute to our suffering and develop new, more useful ways of being and operating. Be patient and kind to yourself as you make the effort to identify areas where there's a need for more personal growth.

It's not simple or easy to become a wise, fulfilled, more fully evolved version of ourselves. Obstacles and difficulties will be encountered along the way. It can be quite challenging to find healthy ways to meet our needs, feel good, and protect ourselves from pain. Both insight and new experience will be needed. The next chapters will supply useful information and guidance for deeper understanding of yourself, and identification of what kind of inner work could improve the quality of your life. You will be encouraged to utilize resources that can support you in the process of taking better care of yourself and your mental health—from reading books and listening to inspiring podcasts, to seeking professional help.

You can learn to love and respect yourself, constructively process thoughts and feelings, be self-aware and insightful, have good relationships, be resilient, and actively influence the direction of your life in positive ways. Useful knowledge, willingness to learn about and invest in your ongoing development, and helpful resources to support your efforts are all part of the essential ingredients for the improved mental health and fulfilling life that I hope you will have.

CHAPTER 3

Your Sense of Self and Its Parts

"There's such a lot of different Annes in me. I sometimes think that is why I'm such a troublesome person. If I was just the one Anne it would be ever so much more comfortable, but then it wouldn't be half so interesting."

—L.M. Montgomery, *Anne of Green Gables*

We live our lives with a general sense of self that reflects our personal, subjective experience of ourselves. You can think of it as *what it is like to be me*. The term "self" captures a sense of personhood that is unique to you.

Our sense of self is largely shaped by our experiences growing up. As children, we internalize the ways in which we're perceived and treated by people who are important to us. We start out in life believing, "I must be who you see me to be." Sometimes that belief morphs into, "I must become who you need me to be." Our developing sense of self is greatly impacted by our interactions with our parents, caregivers, teachers, peers, and society.

Influence of Caregivers on Our Sense of Self

As we grow up, our need to be loved, valued, and accepted is quite powerful. So much so that to ensure our caregivers will accept and care for us, we typically mold ourselves into what our caregivers need us to be or can handle. Feeling the need to accommodate what our parents or caregivers need, prefer, or can tolerate limits our opportunities to fully explore and express parts of ourselves that don't feel welcome or safe enough to emerge.

If you're lucky, you grow up feeling seen, understood, valued, loved, and encouraged. You're allowed to be yourself and explore your natural interests. Under those conditions, you begin to develop a healthy sense of self. You believe in your inherent worth and have the freedom to discover yourself—what you like (desires), what you're capable of (talents and strengths), what you need to work on (shortcomings), what matters to you (values), and what kind of life you hope to create for yourself (hopes, goals). You believe you matter because you're treated as if you matter. You generally have faith in yourself and appreciate that you have something unique to offer the world.

If unlucky, you may have been raised by people who had poor self-esteem themselves or were struggling to get through each day. Their own difficulties made it hard for them to appreciate or accept you. You may have experienced varying degrees of abuse or neglect. Unfortunately, many of us didn't grow up in environments that brought out the best in us or helped us feel comfortable with ourselves.

If your caregivers don't have the time, ability, or interest in being appropriately responsive to you, it's hard not to feel devalued, uninteresting, or unimportant. Without someone to reflect back that a lovable and interesting person is emerging, you may feel like you don't matter or you're unlovable. This was Sophia's experience, so she silenced herself and ignored her bad feelings to avoid disturbing her parents. She even shut down good feelings like excitement because they also seemed unwelcome. Sometimes, the environment you grow up in doesn't leave you enough safety or room to live as your full authentic self. You learn to disavow parts of yourself to avoid upsetting your caregivers or being shamed by them. Without enough recognition and attunement from your caregivers, you may become invisible not only to them but also to yourself.

> Your sense of self can keep evolving over time, as you continue to develop into the fullest version of yourself possible.

The good news is that eventually, as you grow older and are less dependent on your caregivers, you can begin to reclaim disavowed parts of yourself. You can develop a sense of self that isn't a reflection of what others think of you or expect you to be but is, instead, rooted in knowing, valuing, loving, working on, and accepting all parts of yourself.

MARCUS'S DEVELOPING SENSE OF SELF

Marcus was an average student whose mom remarried when he was ten years old to a stepfather who berated him for his less-than-stellar grades. He can still hear the man's voice echoing in his head, "How could you be so stupid? What's wrong with you? You'll never amount to anything!" His stepdad constantly compared Marcus to his older half-brother, who was exceptionally smart, athletic, and excelled at school. Marcus felt like a chronic disappointment, never good enough. His mom encouraged him to be tolerant of his stepdad because she believed he meant well, but her advice left him feeling like he wasn't worth standing up for or protecting.

Harshness as a form of motivation doesn't work as well as expecting and encouraging your child's best effort. Harsh criticism tends to make kids feel small and inadequate, whereas encouragement of and praise for effort makes them feel capable and empowered.[1] Marcus's stepdad used fear, criticism, and comparisons as motivation, leaving Marcus feeling increasingly more anxious, insecure, and inadequate. His stepfather's focus on his "failures" and "shortcomings" made it increasingly difficult for Marcus to believe in or feel good about himself and develop confidence. He vaguely remembers early years when he liked school and wasn't so terrified of making mistakes, which is a normal process of learning and improving. Sadly, Marcus's stepfather didn't seem to care much about his efforts, and he seemed unaware of the reality that the outcome of a child's effort will vary depending on their strengths and aptitudes.

Together Marcus and I explored how his stepdad's approach to parenting had damaged his self-esteem, and he began untangling himself from the most toxic messages he absorbed. Marcus came to understand that his stepdad was intolerant of his "averageness" because he believed it reflected poorly on him—as if all his children should be just as smart and capable as he was. Over time, he rebuilt confidence in his own unique capabilities, which didn't include being a straight-A student.

MARIE'S DEVELOPING SENSE OF SELF

Marie encountered her own problems with parents who had unrelenting expectations that she be outstanding. She was smart and quite capable, excelling at everything she did, but her upbringing conditioned her to believe love was conditional, only available when she met her parents' highest expectations. Whenever she fell short, they withdrew their attention and affection. Their disappointment in her was searingly painful, so she set out to avoid it by only allowing the most impressive or perfect parts of herself to show.

Marie ended up becoming quite the overachiever. In her world, there was only room for one person on top. She became so competitive with others she found it hard to make and keep friends or bond with co-workers. Part of her wanted to be happy for others when they succeeded and be a team player, but she felt threatened by others' successes. To feel secure or good about herself, she had to be "the best."

When Marie began therapy, the idea of inherent self-worth was foreign to her. Experience taught her that to maintain attention or feel valued, she needed to be a superstar. Not just really good, but better than others. While she had an impressive list of external achievements and awards, she felt deeply unhappy and alone. We worked together to dismantle unhealthy narratives from her childhood and build a better foundation for healthy self-esteem and self-worth—one sturdy enough to include cheering on others. Slowly, Marie became able to see herself as a worthwhile human being, apart from perfectionism, superiority, and accomplishments. She came to see the value of living more authentically, rather than performatively.

Influence of the Social Environment on Your Sense of Self

Beyond our home environments, our developing sense of self is also influenced by the ways we are seen and treated by society and our peers. Most societies exhibit some form of social stratification resembling a caste system, where status is allocated based on various factors such as gender, wealth, religion, ancestry, race, occupation, or education. It can be hard to value yourself if society, without truly knowing you, devalues or disregards you based on one of these characteristics.

Starting in early adolescence, there's a natural shift from primary reliance on family for support to reliance on peer groups for acceptance. We desperately want to be liked and to fit in. As a result, we often abandon the most authentic expressions of ourselves out of fear of rejection.

Social media further complicates the development of healthy self-esteem and puts enormous pressure on us to meet unrealistic standards set by the most attractive, popular, or successful people of the moment. You're inundated with pictures of others presenting themselves in their best light, living their best lives, with thousands of friends or followers—image after curated image. It's fertile ground for feelings of inferiority, inadequacy, and envy. Research shows a correlation between the rise in social media and eating disorders, increased body dissatisfaction, and the desire for plastic surgery.[2]

Young folks especially need extra compassion and support navigating the development of healthy self-esteem with the influence of social media starting at such a young age. Constant access to comparisons can leave them feeling "less than." If you're learning how to accept and appreciate your unique self, viewing others' curated social media feeds typically makes it harder to feel satisfied with your regular, still evolving, and sometimes awkward self. When you long to be recognized, you may be tempted to do and post things just to get attention, any attention. Sometimes those posts aren't well thought out and don't align with your most authentic self or best interests. Conditional attention also evaporates quickly and feels empty compared to being noticed and liked for simply being you.

It's easier, as well, for people to perform acts of cruelty online.[3] Becoming the object of gossip, teasing, or rejection can harm and derail a young person's developing sense of self, something that's still quite tenuous and vulnerable to attacks. Abuse from peers can evoke painful feelings and beliefs that you are inadequate, unacceptable, ugly, weird, unlovable, or just not good enough. Anonymity makes us less accountable because there's a lack of real-time feedback, meaning we don't actually see how we've hurt someone.

Unfortunately, the urge to hurt others can be very strong, and many people are dealing with a variety of difficult circumstances without sufficient resources. If they haven't found healthier ways to cope with their own inner turmoil, they're likely to discharge it by acting out their pain on others. A lot of cruelty is dished out during formative school-age years, a tumultuous and vulnerable time of life when many young people aren't fully equipped to handle their distress and negative feelings maturely, nor are they well equipped to deal with being the object of others' pain and aggression. Our youth are in dire need of compassion and support as they navigate some of these challenges and search for ways to constructively address acts of cruelty.

I encourage you to compassionately work through any difficult experiences you had growing up that negatively shaped how you think of yourself. Yet even if those experiences and messages negatively impacted your view of yourself, they do not have the final word on who you really are or who you can become.

Parts of Our Selves

Your sense of self might feel like one single entity, but a growing body of research and clinical experience points to a more nuanced understanding of the self as dynamic and multifaceted, possessing multiple, context-dependent self-aspects that emerge in response to varying social roles, relationships, and contexts. We are influenced by a multiplicity of parts[4] or different self-states[5,6]. Having a healthy sense of self includes being able to live more fully as your entire, authentic self, without disavowing the parts of yourself that you are ashamed of or dislike.

> Our most authentic sense of self is made up of multiple parts. Embrace them all.

The term "self-state" refers to the current state of mind you are in at any given moment. It includes certain feelings, reactions, beliefs, and thoughts that tend to be activated, or awakened, under certain conditions. For instance, if you are good at something and you're in an environment where your competencies can shine, a confident self-state may be activated. The opposite holds true if you are in a context where you've had bad experiences. A more fearful or insecure self-state may become activated. This is because we hold memories of past experiences. When we are in similar situations, it's not uncommon for the self-states (feelings, thoughts, behaviors, expectations) that grew out of the original good or bad experience to become reactivated. But the self-state is more than just an old memory. It also includes feelings, beliefs, and bodily sensations that feel quite alive in the present.

Some self-states are so familiar to us that they earn a name or label. Some common examples are: likeable or "good" me, "bad" me, younger me, protector, vulnerable me, critic, worrier, controller/manager, task master, comfort craver, grumpy me, optimist, wise me, warrior, loving me, etc. Each part tends to operate from its own set of needs, agendas, beliefs, feelings, and capacities. Try to approach different parts of yourself with acceptance and curiosity—learn what they represent about you and your life experience. It also helps to be aware of and identify what circumstances tend to activate different parts of yourself.

You aren't always of one mind, which can make life feel a bit complicated. It's important to understand what each part of yourself is trying to express or accomplish and learn to notice which part of yourself is in the driver's seat at any given moment, directing your thoughts, feelings, or behaviors. Ultimately, you want to develop a "Wise Self" part as the most prominent governing force within you so it can take the wheel when another part is running the show but causing problems, despite good intentions. Some parts of you will need extra help finding alternative ways to express themselves and more constructive ways to meet their needs.

When Sophia is in the presence of chips or sweets, a childlike part of her wants to indulge without limits. She feels excited and free.

Food was one of the few things she had some control over when she was young. She could comfort or reward herself with snacks without having to involve others who were unavailable or unreliable. Yet another part of Sophia, her manager/controlling part, is determined to feed her body more nutritious food and maintain a healthy weight. Those two parts have conflicting agendas and needs. She slowly experimented with new ways to comfort and reward herself, like taking a bubble bath, going for a walk, and talking to someone, so that food wasn't her only outlet available for pleasure or coping with bothersome thoughts and feelings. She could try to meet her need for comfort in a way that didn't interfere with another competing need: good health.

Alexander, another patient, had a co-worker who periodically embarrassed him by teasing or criticizing him during team meetings. His protector part was furious and wanted to retaliate. Yet another part of him knew that acting aggressively or losing his cool would result in costly consequences. Over time, Alexander experimented with different ways to constructively deal with this co-worker that included asserting firmer boundaries and skillfully confronting his co-worker. His aggressive protector part wasn't needed when he was able to be skillfully assertive instead.

It's not uncommon to have different parts of ourselves activated simultaneously, each part exhibiting different levels of maturity, emotionality, rationality, needs, and coping strategies. The different needs and reactions reflected by different parts of yourself help explain why it can be extra challenging at times to address your needs.

Remember that no part or self-state reflects all of who you are—it simply represents an activated aspect of yourself. You're much more than whatever current thoughts, feelings, behaviors, or moods are in the foreground at any given moment. Understanding, working with, and integrating the complex and rich parts that make up your sense of self is an important aspect of creating good mental health.

Exercise: Identify Experiences That Shaped You and Your Ways of Being

For the sake of deeper self-awareness, consider writing responses to the following questions to understand what influenced the development of your sense of self and shaped your autopilot beliefs, patterns, expectations, coping strategies, and ways of operating that are now part of your conscious and unconscious mind. Some of the answers may not be immediately accessible but can become clearer as you make the effort to better understand yourself and your history.

1. How was your view of yourself and others influenced by the way that your caregivers, peers, relatives, and teachers/coaches treated you? Include both the affirming and belittling or negative messages you absorbed about yourself. What did their behavior teach you about others?

2. As a child, what aspects of yourself (feelings, desires, beliefs, behaviors, or characteristics) were most welcomed? What parts of yourself did you feel you had to hide, disavow, or reject?

3. What attitudes and beliefs (positive and negative) did you learn growing up that organize the way you tend to see the world? For

example, is your worldview fairly optimistic and hopeful or did your experiences leave you feeling more pessimistic or fearful?

4. What did you learn about giving and receiving love and care while growing up? Common ways of demonstrating love are acts of service, words of affirmation, gifts, quality time, and physical touch. How did your family members show love, positive regard, and affection?

5. What did you learn about forming connections with others? Were positive, reliable forms of attachment available? Did your interactions with your caregivers generally leave you feeling secure (confident, trusting), or did inconsistencies in their availability or a lack of warmth or safety leave you feeling more anxious (insecure, clinging), avoidant (detached), or disorganized (fearful, confused)? Insight into your attachment style and new opportunities for healthier relating give you a chance to develop a secure attachment style later in life (earned secure attachment).

6. How did you learn to handle conflict and anger (e.g., fight back, be passive, be aggressive, avoid conflict, be assertive, talk things through until some compromise or understanding was reached)? How did others in your family handle conflict?

7. How were disappointments and losses handled? What did you learn about grieving? Were losses in your life acknowledged and responded to with empathy? What were some difficult losses in your life, and have you processed and worked through them?

8. What are the coping strategies you resorted to in order to protect yourself from pain and disappointment or other unwanted feelings (e.g., denial, substance or alcohol use, eating, rationalizations,

retail therapy, working out, being in nature, prayer, writing, reaching out for help, etc.)? Identify the coping strategies you relied upon the most—the healthy ones and the ones that can cause problems in your life and need upgrading.

9. What values did your family encourage, model, or live by (e.g., excellence, hard work, obedience, learning, freedom, generosity, integrity, resilience, adventure, connection, collaboration, productivity, spirituality, etc.)? (See the Appendix for a Values Clarification Exercise.)

Sometimes this exercise can evoke uncomfortable feelings, especially if you're reminded of the ways your childhood was disappointing. You may need time and help to compassionately mourn the losses and disappointments coming into your awareness.

CHAPTER 4

A Healthy Sense of Self

"Always remember you matter, and you bring to this world what no one else does."

—Charlie Mackesy

Our sense of self develops out of years of experiences. Hopefully you received a lot of affirming messages about yourself. The more troublesome beliefs about ourselves typically stem from harmful messages we absorbed during childhood, due to being treated poorly by others or inadequate care. It can take time to work through the impact—especially if the negative comments were forcefully or repeatedly delivered. Tend to the psychological wounds you carry; otherwise, those wounds can infect and undermine your sense of self.

Your sense of self is not fixed. As you strive to understand and develop yourself, it's useful to have some balance between accepting yourself as you are and encouraging yourself to evolve into the best versions of you that you can be.[1]

Let's start by examining what a healthy sense of self looks like.

What a Healthy Sense of Self Includes

SELF-AWARENESS

You have a deep understanding of yourself and how you developed. You're curious about why you think, behave, and feel as you do. You're honest with yourself about what you observe, and you make use of that knowledge. You are aware of your autopilot tendencies—how you protect yourself, get your needs met, deal with difficulties and conflict, and relate to others. You mindfully notice what's going on with yourself without excessive judgment or criticism.

SELF-ESTEEM

You value yourself and *appreciate your strengths*, good qualities, capabilities, and accomplishments. Self-esteem emerges from a combination of self-worth—the belief that you have inherent value, that you matter, that you're worthy of love and respect independent of external circumstances or accomplishments—and a sense of mastery, the development of skills and abilities to effectively navigate life.

Healthy esteem includes the ability to feel proud of yourself without being arrogant or acting entitled and superior (e.g., narcissism), while also having enough humility to acknowledge that you'll make mistakes and have shortcomings. You accept the whole package of who you are, your positive traits as well as your flaws. Research shows that self-acceptance correlates closely with being happy and satisfied with life overall.[2]

While self-esteem is affected by how we're seen and evaluated by others, it's important to not let others' opinions of you solely dictate how you feel about yourself. Try not to dwell on how you compare to others. Spend your energy, instead, becoming the best version of you that you can be, someone you like and respect. (See the Appendix for an exercise on Identifying Your Strengths and Positive Qualities.)

AUTHENTICITY

You're *free to be yourself, your full authentic self.* You pay attention to what your truest desires, values, strengths, and preferences are, and you let them guide you. By contrast, some people develop what we call a "false self," an identity based primarily on what others expect you to be or what you think will win you favor, status, and attention.

Social media invites people to present performative and curated versions of themselves, which doesn't typically include the fullness of who you really are and exacerbates the fear that only the best or most interesting aspects of yourself are lovable or worthy of attention. Living as your authentic self helps reduce the temptation to compare yourself to others or live a life of imitation. You encourage yourself to accept and appreciate who you uniquely are, and you do what you can to keep evolving into your fullest, most authentic self.

Living authentically also includes reclaiming and integrating parts of yourself you've previously disavowed or hidden. You learn to embrace the richness of who you are and all you've been through, and you accept that different parts of you get activated depending on the circumstances.

AGENCY AND ENCOURAGEMENT

You believe in your capacity to influence your life, your thoughts, feelings, actions, and attitudes. You're assertive and you advocate for what matters. You speak up for your rights while respecting others' rights. You act with intention to direct and influence the course of your life.

You willingly use whatever resources you have within and around you to face and deal with hard things. You redirect yourself when you're off track and motivate yourself with encouragement and determination rather than punishment, criticism, or harshness.[3] You also actively develop and seek out a variety of healthy ways to feel good and bring pleasure into your life, which makes you less vulnerable to some of the more addictive sources of feeling good. You see yourself as an important co-creator of your reality.

CORE VALUES AND A MORAL COMPASS

You have a sense of right and wrong that allows you to successfully live within society's norms, get along with others, and develop integrity. You lead a values-driven life, aligning your actions with what matters most, which contributes to a sense of purpose and meaning. Your values are key to a healthy mind and self, which leads to increased fulfillment and overall well-being.[4]

Higher-level functioning requires we base moral reasoning on internalized principles and awareness of the impact our decisions have on others. Guilt signals us to reappraise our behaviors and redirect ourselves as needed, but guilt needs to be tempered by appropriate amounts of patience and forgiveness with our humanness and mistakes. Core values play an important role in our choices and decision-making and help provide motivation to sacrifice immediate gratification for the sake of longer-term goals.

COMPASSION

You're compassionate with yourself and respond with appropriate care and concern when life is hard and you're in pain. You make an effort to be there for yourself at those times in the way you would be for a good friend. You start by listening, trying to understand and empathize, and offer some comfort.

Some people fear that self-compassion will make them soft, weak, or ineffective. Instead, research shows cultivating self-compassion actually enhances your ability to think things through and consider options for coping.[5] It's important to develop healthy ways to comfort and take good care of yourself, but that doesn't mean you ignore the ways you may be contributing to your difficulties. You can be kind to yourself when you're hurting and still acknowledge that you have things to work on.

MEANING AND PURPOSE

You develop a sense of direction, meaning, and purpose for your life. Your interests, strengths, values, and personal philosophy guide you and help you hold the "big picture" of your life in mind—your hopes for the ways your life will matter to you and to others. We don't have to change the world or solve life's biggest problems to make meaningful contributions. Find your own unique way to add something meaningful and useful to the world, no matter how small.

Balancing Self-Acceptance and Change

With regards to self-improvement, striking a balance between accepting ourselves as we are and encouraging ourselves to change and evolve is important. As you attempt to understand, develop, and integrate all parts of yourself, you may benefit from professional help. Therapy is one way to work through unresolved issues interfering with a healthy sense of self, such as shame, excessive self-criticism and social comparisons, or beliefs that you're only lovable or worthy if you're "x, y, or z."

Regardless of how you approach your journey of personal growth and development, be patient with the process. Try to avoid the extremes of unrelenting and perfectionistic pursuit at one end, or defeatist collapse or apathy at the other. Be aware that on any given day, depending on your state of mind and circumstances, you'll have more or less energy to push yourself toward your goals and be your best self. Take advantage of good energy days and practice patience on difficult ones.

When you catch yourself feeling jealous, inadequate, or disappointed as you witness others thriving or enjoying aspects of life that aren't currently going as well for you, have compassion for yourself but don't let those feelings consume you. Let others' successes inspire you to keep working on yourself and your life. Focus on reaching your potential and practicing gratitude for what's good in your life to help alleviate jealousy or envy.

Remember: Personal growth and transformation aren't easy for many reasons. Early determinants of who we are and who we became (influences from our genetics, environment, culture, life events, and circumstances) become deeply embedded over time. It can be scary to let go of old ways of protecting yourself or depart from what's familiar to venture into the unknowns of change.

Being criticized or made fun of when you take a risk can make you not want to try at all. If your caregivers criticized you for trying to do something and doing it poorly, you may have learned to give up at the first sign of difficulty. Making changes can feel risky, but it's pretty hard to be good at something you haven't yet mastered through trial and error and practice. Relying on avoidance to protect yourself minimizes the likelihood of embarrassment, humiliation, and disappointment—but at a huge cost.

For example, my patient Alexander relied on avoidance to cope with his mother's constant fault-finding. She scrutinized everything he did. He eventually told himself that he didn't have to feel bad about failing if he avoided putting himself in positions to fail. What he needed and didn't get was help developing the resilience to bounce back from mistakes and failures. He didn't get the needed encouragement and support to develop a growth mindset, which would have allowed him to try new things and be willing to look bad in the process—a normal part of learning and getting better at something.[6]

If you experienced trauma growing up and haven't had an opportunity to process the impact it had on you, then you'll likely find it difficult to make changes because your mindset is focused on staying safe. You may have developed self-protective mechanisms to survive dire circumstances. Parts of yourself found ways to guard you very carefully, and to this day, those parts resist giving up their important jobs.

Change requires developing parts of yourself that can protect you without constricting possibilities for a full life. It involves gaining awareness and working through unpleasant memories, which can feel threatening. Yet, with the right kind of help, healing and change is possible. However, just because personal growth is good for you doesn't mean it'll come easily. It takes courage to change and grow, so bring a mixture of acceptance, willingness, patience, perseverance, and compassion with you. Expect change to be an uneven process that is neither fast nor permanent. Make space for both acceptance and change.

Self-Talk: What Parts of Yourself Speak Loudest?

If there was ever a relationship you should care about improving, it should be the relationship you have with yourself. You cannot escape your own company! We're with ourselves 24/7, so make the relationship you have to yourself, all parts of yourself, healthy.

> Make sure your relationship with yourself is good.
> Be your own best friend and wise counsel.

The way you talk to yourself, to your different parts, dramatically affects your mood, motivation, decisions, feelings, and self-esteem. This is referred to as self-talk. Ideally, your tone will be wise, kind, and encouraging as often as possible, even when you're facing mistakes you've made or are dealing with your shortcomings. Remember, encouragement is a better motivator than harshness.

Imagine you just said something mean to a friend in anger. Do you say to yourself, "Wow, I wonder why you said that. It was really uncalled for and hurt them badly. Why am I so angry right now? How can I make amends?" Or are you more likely to say, "You idiot! You just ruined that relationship. You are such a loser!"

Learn to use language that motivates you to investigate your behaviors, to do better next time, and to repair the problem, rather than simply berating or shaming yourself. Question yourself with curiosity. Practice redirecting inner dialogue that becomes consumed with anxiety, negativity, hostility, or pessimism. For example, when you are experiencing a lot of fear, don't let fear be the only voice in your head that gets airtime.

Changing self-talk requires persistent effort and multiple strategies. It helps to understand where your current self-talk tendencies come from: Why does your inner dialogue sound so mean, critical, perfectionist, defeatist, scared, or pessimistic? Recognize what part of yourself is talking. Is the current voice in your head coming from a frightened younger part, or your rebellious teenager part, or your angry protector part? It's all right to hear them out, but you don't want certain voices to drown out other wiser input.

Redirect internal conversation when you catch yourself talking to yourself in ways that are unproductive or mean, accelerate anxiety, or are disrespectful.

1. Pause and take a deep breath.
2. Then say to yourself, "Those comments aren't helpful."

Start over, speaking to yourself as you would a good friend or someone else you care about and want to help. Strive to make the climate and conversation in your head a welcoming, calmer, inviting, discerning, and nurturing environment as often as possible.

Parts of Your Self to Cultivate

In this Information Age, when we're inundated with data but relatively few sources seem to offer real wisdom, it's all the more important to develop and nurture inner wisdom to rely on.

Most of us would benefit immensely from developing three parts of ourselves to play more prominent roles in guiding us through life: a Wise Self, a Warrior Self, and a Loving Self. These parts can become leading forces in our hearts and minds.

DEVELOPING YOUR WISE SELF

Your Wise Self offers thoughtful council, discernment, and empathy and is intent upon understanding and appreciating your experience at any given moment—to help you make sense of what's happening and direct you toward useful responses. This part of you embraces your feelings when you're hurting or overwhelmed by your emotions; yet, at the same time, it also considers input from the more rational and practical part of your mind.[7] By staying steady and calm, it helps you address your state of mind and present concerns in ways that are constructive, effective, and supportive of your overall well-being.

Wise Self also holds you accountable without being overly harsh or demeaning because it embodies your best, most aspirational qualities and capacities. Wise Self acts as a caring and thoughtful best friend, mentor, mediator, caregiver, and advisor within, available to consult with at all times. The Wise Self mediates between different parts of yourself and is interested in what each part needs and holds in mind the big picture, while sorting through the complexity of your experience.

While conceptualizing and developing a Wise Self, some of my patients have found it helpful to think of people in their lives who embody the characteristics they desire to cultivate. One patient envisioned his grandmother as part of his Wise Self. She helped raise him after his mother died when he was five, and she was the kindest and most insightful person he knew. She was loving and understanding but never afraid to question him if he behaved poorly or seemed out of sorts. She could confront him with gentleness and genuine curiosity as to how he had gotten off track. She was caring, real, direct, and trustworthy.

Another patient thought of her Wise Self as the part of her that God spoke through, a higher power whom she experienced as strong, wise, and benevolent. Jamie, a different patient, envisioned his basketball coach as the model for his Wise Self, a man who had faced many challenges in his life but remained a beacon of strength, kindness, integrity, and wisdom to his players and community. Initially, he found it easier to imagine the voice of his coach as the Wise Self within him, rather than his own voice. One of my patients decided to rename their Wise Self as Superhero Self. Do what works for you to develop and connect with a wise, caring, honest, steady, and strong internal force within you.

AWAKENING WARRIOR SELF

Think of Warrior Self as representing the part of you that aims to be brave and courageous in the face of fear or difficulties. It represents your sense of determination, perseverance, grit, and resilience. When you're in a jam, your Warrior Self helps you find the energy and strength you'll need to face whatever challenge is before you.

Your Warrior Self lives by the motto, "We can deal with hard things." And you can develop these capabilities, even if they currently seem in short supply. To awaken and connect with your developing Warrior Self, it helps to remember times in your life when you faced and got through a difficulty, or imagine people in your life who've faced and bounced back from terrible adversity. Channel their courage and resilience through you until it feels like your own.

CULTIVATING YOUR LOVING SELF

Loving Self represents the part of us that is capable of love, kindness, compassion, and passion. If you felt unloved for much of your life, it'll take more work for you to develop this part of yourself, but don't be deterred. Love enriches our lives in so many ways: It facilitates healing and personal growth and improves our relationships with ourselves and others. If necessary, get help figuring out why you may struggle to feel entitled or worthy of love and kindness. A kind and loving relationship with yourself enhances your ability to be loving and supportive of others. Love has a way of bringing out the best in all of us, so everyone wins with more love.

Together, these parts of yourself remind you to tap into your growing wisdom, strength, and love. The cluster of qualities they represent can help replace less helpful ways you learned to get by in life. Keep nurturing and reawakening these life-enhancing parts of yourself.

You're worth every effort you make to further develop yourself and create a healthier sense of self. It helps to understand what shaped your current sense of self, so you can recover from past negative influences and strengthen parts of yourself, qualities, and capabilities that contribute to a healthier sense of self moving forward. If you need to, get proper help to work through any psychological wounds (unresolved and lingering pain, insecurities, or shame) you still carry that negatively impact the way you view and experience yourself. Your sense of self has a tremendous impact on how you think, feel, and approach life, so make it a priority to learn how to love and appreciate yourself, live authentically, and use your agency to build a good life and relationships.

EXERCISE: SELF-ASSESSMENT OF A HEALTHY SENSE OF SELF

Use this self-assessment to identify the capacities you'd like to work on for personal growth and to improve your mental health. These affirming statements remind you of what you are capable of or are working toward. Rate each statement on a scale of 1 to 3:

1 = needs attention
2 = making progress or "good enough"
3 = this is a strength

SELF-AWARENESS

____ I have a deep understanding of myself and how I came to be who I am.

____ I'm aware of how I tend to protect myself, get my needs met, deal with difficulties and conflict, and show love.

____ I reflect on my experience and try to make sense of it.

____ I can be honest with myself without being overly harsh or critical.

____ I use self-awareness to learn from my experience, redirect myself, heal, and grow.

SELF-ESTEEM

____ I accept, love, and value myself.

____ I have a sense of pride for my efforts, accomplishments, competencies, and positive characteristics.

____ I have enough humility to admit when I'm wrong or misguided, and I'm aware of and willing to work on my shortcomings.

____ I use encouragement and supportive self-talk to motivate myself, instead of berating or belittling myself.

____ I compassionately face and work through the reasons I feel insecure, guilty, or ashamed.

____ I'm doing my best to not excessively compare myself to others.

____ I accept who I am, an imperfect human, while doing what I can to develop myself into all of who I'm capable of becoming.

____ I talk to myself the same way I would to a friend I value, respect, and care about.

AUTHENTICITY

____ I feel free to be my most authentic self.

____ I'm careful not to sacrifice important parts of myself to be what others expect or want me to be, especially if it doesn't resonate with who I really am or want to be.

____ I accept all parts of myself, not just the most likeable parts.

____ I welcome back hidden or disavowed parts of myself, so I can feel more integrated and whole.

____ I resist living as a "false self," showing only the best, most curated version of myself.

AGENCY

____ I intentionally direct and influence my life in positive ways.

____ I know myself well enough to advocate for and pursue what matters to me.

____ I'm assertive.

____ I'm willing to face and deal with hard things.

____ I redirect myself as needed, using encouragement and discipline.

____ I have multiple, healthy ways of bringing pleasure into my everyday life, so I'm not too dependent on any one source of pleasure that could become an addiction.

CORE VALUES AND A MORAL COMPASS

____ I have values and principles that guide my choices and decisions.

____ I align my actions with what truly matters, not just for the moment, but for the long run too.

____ I have a sense of right and wrong that allows me to cooperatively live in society with others.

____ I have empathy for others.

____ I learn from my mistakes and make amends when necessary.

COMPASSION

____ I meet my own suffering, and the suffering of others, with a kind, attentive presence and a spirit of compassionate responsiveness.

____ I can comfort and take good care of myself when I'm having a rough time.

MEANING AND PURPOSE

____ I find ways to live with a sense of purpose, orienting my life around personally meaningful values and goals.

____ I find meaning in my life and significance derived from connecting with and contributing to something larger than myself.

WISE, WARRIOR, AND LOVING SELF

____ I appreciate and rely on the parts of me that are capable of being wise, insightful, honest, empathic, loving, kind, encouraging, courageous, and resilient.

____ I allow the Wise Self to lead and mediate between the other parts of myself.

BALANCE OF ACCEPTANCE AND CHANGE

____ I'm finding balance between accepting myself as I am and making efforts to work on aspects of myself that could use some attention and refinement.

CHAPTER 5

Mental Capacities

"The mind is its own place, and in itself can make a heaven of hell, a hell of heaven."

—John Milton

Three important psychological capacities—mental, emotional, and relational—are needed for good mental health, and this chapter will focus on mental capacities (the next two chapters will cover emotional and relational capacities). Different factors, such as environmental influences and epigenetics, play a role in how easy or hard it might be to develop certain psychological capacities. The most straightforward way to develop your psychological capacities is to learn them experientially, with guidance from others, while growing up.

We internalize the ways we're treated by and interact with our caregivers and significant others. If our caregivers are curious about what we feel and think, show compassion when we are hurting, and help us think through and cope with difficulties, we internalize that shared experience and develop the capacity to soothe ourselves, regulate our emotions, plan and problem-solve, and be observant of and interested in our states of mind. We awaken and develop an attitude of care and curiosity about ourselves and, by extension, others too. We internalize and develop the capacity to tolerate and make meaning of the full range of our experiences because someone offered that kind of responsiveness to us at an age when we weren't yet capable of providing it for ourselves.

However, it's difficult for caregivers to offer something to their children that they haven't yet developed or did not get themselves when they were young. As such, most of us will have to work on further developing some aspects of these psychological capacities that weren't sufficiently awakened and developed during our childhood, as most humans are raised in imperfect conditions.

Understanding Mental Capacities

Our thinking, rational mind plays a critical role in our lives. Mental capacities allow us to be self-reflective and discerning, notice and consider multiple aspects of a situation, use good judgment, make meaning of our experiences, and gain insights about ourselves and others. They give us the ability to navigate life more effectively and meaningfully. Some of the most important mental capacities we need for good mental health develop in a part of the brain called the prefrontal cortex, which is responsible for what scientists call "executive functioning"—the ability to plan, manage time, delay gratification, regulate emotions and behavior, and adapt to change. The prefrontal cortex operates as an air traffic control tower in our brain.

The prefrontal cortex most actively develops between adolescence and age 25. This explains why children and adolescents often act impulsively without much thought for consequences. Early on, we rely on others to help us develop these executive-functioning or mental capacities. Research shows that the development of the prefrontal cortex is compromised in people who were raised in impoverished and adverse environments, where they were treated poorly or deprived of adequate care.[1]

> Mental capacities help us behave with greater intention, responding thoughtfully rather than simply reacting without thinking.

Caregivers help us develop these mental capacities when they reflect with us so we can learn from our experiences. If caregivers react with anger or shaming before any other calmer discussion and exploration of a mistake or undesired behavior occurs, children typically shut down and are left alone with their feelings of guilt, fear, shame, or anger. Children learn to not share their problems or mistakes for fear of how grown-ups will respond, which equates to lost opportunities. In these cases, children don't learn to reflect on their behaviors and choices, to see what kinds of consequences come from certain actions or understand how their behaviors impact others.

When, on the other hand, caregivers walk children through incidents in a way that helps them process what happened, they learn to put their minds to good use. These children tend to become thoughtful and self-reflective because they had someone to show them how to self-reflect and make meaning of their experiences. As these children mature, they can consider possible consequences of their actions before they act.

Fortunately, the brain is capable of changing, and you can improve mental capacities that were insufficiently developed while growing up.

Mental capacities include the following abilities: self-reflection and insight, observing your mind, focus and attention, and good judgment and strategic planning. We'll dive a bit deeper into each of these.

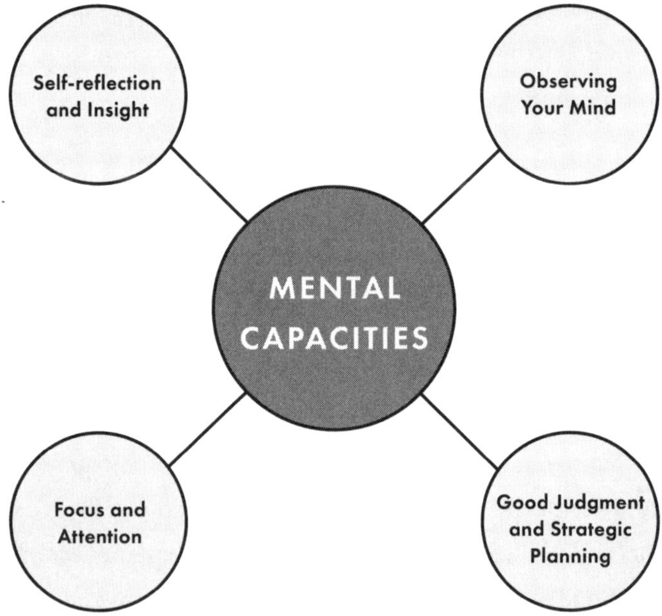

SELF-REFLECTION AND INSIGHT

One of the most important mental capacities is the ability to reflect on and make sense of your experiences. When you do, you tend to feel less confused and overwhelmed. Having a better understanding of what's going on also helps with problem-solving. If you feel overcome by a wave of intense feelings or have an urge to behave poorly—there's a reason. You want to be able to slow down and make sense of what is going on with you, rather than feel at the mercy of mysterious forces.

Asking yourself a few questions can help you reflect on and gain some useful insights:

- Why am I feeling or behaving this way?
- What stories am I telling myself about what is going on?
- What is the meaning of my current obsession, feeling, or mood?
- What does this experience bring up for me or remind me of?

In trying to make sense of your experiences, you learn to notice and investigate the thoughts, needs, attitudes, and stories contributing to the way you're feeling, acting, or perceiving. You're capable of seeing how past experience colors the present moment. You're open to questioning yourself, noticing the times when the information you digest and the stories you tell yourself may be inaccurate, unhealthy, or misleading. In this way, you can thoughtfully evaluate which thoughts, beliefs, and narratives could be contributing to your distress and problems.

When my patients fixate on beliefs and stories about themselves or others that seem limiting or irrational, I first try to fully understand their particular perspective. Then, I may respectfully encourage them, as they're willing, to broaden their current understanding and assumptions. While respecting their need to form their own opinions, I hope to foster mental flexibility so those patients can consider multiple possibilities and change their minds when additional information inspires them to be more open-minded.

Most people respond better when they feel heard and understood. Reflecting on your own and others' mental states and intentions, to better understand yourself and them, is called "mentalization." Insight that provides a better understanding of what is going on inside of you and others improves your relationships.

OBSERVING YOUR MIND

Another vital mental capacity is the ability to witness and be curious about your experience from an observational perspective. This is called "metacognition": Rather than be hijacked by your current experience, you have the ability to take a step back and notice thoughts and feelings as they arise. You can simultaneously have an experience while also observing it with curiosity—watching it unfold without being consumed by it.

Let's say a friend makes a comment that seems unkind and you feel hurt and angry. Observing that, you may think, "Wow, I'm having a really strong reaction to my friend's comment. I wonder why she said that, what she means by it, and what it's bringing up for me?" When you separate yourself a little from the immediate onslaught of thoughts and feelings you can try to make sense of what's going on and decide how to respond. If you learn to slow yourself down in those moments, press pause, and regulate your emotions, that helps create the necessary mental space to be curious about what's happening and it tempers reactivity.

Be patient with yourself as you're learning this skill, as it's extra challenging to observe yourself and think things through when you're experiencing intense emotions that can temporarily override your capacity to think. Certain feelings, like fear and anger, activate rapid responses stemming from the brain's limbic system—fight, flight, fawn, or freeze—often before your rational mind has time to process the experience. There are survival benefits to the brain functioning this way. When you are in actual, immediate danger (e.g., a lion is about to pounce and make you its dinner), reacting quickly could save your life. But most of the time, you're better served by taking a few deep breaths so you can more thoughtfully respond rather than simply react to perceived threats.

You'll want to find a balance between using this observational skill to minimize being overtaken by troublesome experiences and allowing yourself enough freedom to be yourself, without constantly observing and evaluating what you're experiencing. You want to be able to be present and engaged with your experience and not be overly self-conscious about what you're saying, doing, thinking, and feeling. Observing ourselves is useful when it enables us to make constructive use of our awareness and positively influence our mental state and responses, and bring a calmer, more curious, and insightful state of mind to certain confusing or dysregulating experiences. The ability to pause and observe what's happening from a distance is helpful when it makes you less at the mercy of a racing mind, intense emotions, and reactivity.

GOOD JUDGMENT AND STRATEGIC PLANNING

Your mind can help you make plans, work toward goals, problem-solve, and adapt to unexpected changes. When you learn from your mistakes, you develop better judgment. You think about the consequences of your actions before making decisions. Good judgment is a critical mental capacity, along with being able to strategize, plan, organize, and manage your time so you can provide direction and structure for your days.

Early on, caregivers are the sources of our executive functioning. Later, we learn how to direct ourselves with intention. Parents who provide the appropriate amount of structure, organization, and routine in children's lives help them internalize good habits and the capacity to do the same for themselves as they become more capable. Caregivers who set appropriate limits, while also having empathy for their children's frustrations, help them develop frustration tolerance.

It's hard to make progress toward building a good life if we don't develop the capacity to use good judgment and strategic planning. We need to be able to tolerate the hard parts of sacrificing immediate gratification to achieve many of our hopes and dreams. If you weren't raised by caregivers who helped you develop these mental capacities, you can develop them later. Wise others—certain friends, therapists, mentors, or spiritual leaders—can help you make progress strengthening these capabilities.

FOCUS AND ATTENTION

Our mind is especially useful to us when we can direct our attention where it's most needed. It can be challenging to stay focused on difficult, boring, or unpleasant tasks, but if we don't learn how to direct our attention, we'll be limited in what we can accomplish in life. Most accomplishments require focused attention to achieve.

Mindfulness and meditation have become increasingly popular ways to train the mind to better focus attention. Research shows that these practices help people to become less reactive and create space for their minds to think things through.[2] Meditation involves focusing your attention on just one thing, such as your breath or a mantra, while allowing other competing thoughts or feelings to pass through your mind without engaging them. Noticeable benefits were found in people doing as little as ten minutes of meditation per day.[3] Mindfulness, on the other hand, is the act of noticing what's going on without judgment by simply observing and naming your experience. For example, you might say to yourself, "I notice anxiety," or "I notice sadness." You simply notice and name the emotional experience, and this nonreactive awareness acts as a clarifying and steadying force.

Mental capacities such as self-reflection and insight, learning to observe yourself, good judgment, focus, and strategic planning enable you to navigate life with greater intention and success.

MIA'S STORY

One of my patients, Mia, started therapy with very few of the mental capacities a person needs and benefits from. Mia's father was a brilliant and demanding tyrant, who couldn't tolerate his children being anything but smart and outstanding, and he had no patience for mistakes. Mia protected herself from his cruelty and denigration with anger and rebellion. By the time she was a teenager, she'd been made a ward of the court and later turned to drugs and alcohol. She became addicted and resorted to prostituting herself and writing bad checks to get by. Eventually, that behavior landed her in jail.

Mia was referred to me after she finished a drug treatment program to help keep her sober and out of jail, but what she really needed was a safe place to heal from traumas, including scars from feeling unlovable and unworthy, as well as being raped and beaten, held at gunpoint, and almost killed over a drug deal that got heated. She needed a trusted person to help her resume development of inner strengths and capacities.

We met multiple times a week for many years, and that journey was both long and eventful. Slowly and unevenly, Mia worked through her pain, overcame significant challenges, and developed missing psychological capacities and a healthier sense of self. Our joint efforts helped her reflect on her experiences, past and present, and she gained valuable insights about herself and others.

Mia had a strong tendency to resort to old coping mechanisms without thinking anything through, which usually aggravated her troubles. Blasting people with anger to protect herself and get them to back off resulted in her being fired from many jobs. She rarely thought about consequences or planned ahead. She was winging it.

Mia gained insight into how critical authority figures reminded her of her father, which helped explain why it took tremendous effort to slow down the initial burst of rage that criticism evoked, rage that had accumulated after many years of being constantly pushed, demeaned, and punished. She slowly learned alternative ways to deal with her anger.

One unusual, albeit creative, idea Mia had was to make a voodoo doll of her boss so she could stick pins in it after work when she was mad at him. I wasn't so sure about that method, but if it kept her from acting unprofessionally or giving her boss a piece of her mind (which never went over well) and getting fired, maybe it was worth a try. Mia didn't get far with the voodoo doll idea, and eventually she found it more helpful to grab a trusted co-worker for a quick chat outside so she could vent a little of her frustration and regroup. She also tried journaling when no one was free to hear her out, and that acted as an emotional release valve.

Mia liked to role-play different ways to respond to tough interpersonal situations. She'd start with freely expressing how upset she felt without putting any pressure on herself to say things carefully. She preferred playing the mean boss or difficult friend, giving me the more challenging task of responding skillfully. After sufficient time in therapy to process her history of disturbing memories and experiences, she found they eventually had less power over her. Her deeper understanding brought important insights and compassion for herself. She slowly became better at reading others and asserting herself without aggression. She learned to make amends when she needed to and eventually began living in a way that fewer amends were needed.

As soon as Mia had steady employment, which took a while, she developed a habit of spending most of her paycheck on clothes that made her feel pretty or look important. She had an overpowering urge to be seen as someone worthy of positive attention. While I expressed empathy for that desire, she and I also explored other ways she could meet her need for respect and recognition, which didn't create additional problems, like the inability to pay her bills (including mine!). It didn't come easily, but over time, Mia began to experience other people treating her with greater kindness and respect—in large part because she now behaved in ways that invited that response. Learning to like and respect herself contributed to better relations with others.

Mia eventually internalized the processes that we regularly engaged in, which included: reflecting on her experience, making sense of it, planning ahead, thinking things through, problem-solving, learning from mistakes without being too ashamed of having made them, using better judgment in the moment to spare herself more pain later, and processing and regulating her emotions.

She learned to observe herself and her situation, and to recognize addictive tendencies before acting on them. I vividly remember one session where Mia proudly told me about the first time she recalled redirecting herself. "There I was, sitting in the car, paycheck in hand, thinking a bunch of things. Do I really want to buy more clothes? Is it worth it? Will I regret it later? Why is this urge so strong today? What am I needing?" I was filled with pride at her curiosity, insight, and capacity for self-reflection. Witnessing her transformation over time was a gift. Mia and I were well aware of all the hard work and painstaking efforts she made to develop capacities that were originally quite limited.

EXERCISE: SELF-ASSESSMENT OF YOUR MENTAL CAPACITIES

Use this self-assessment to identify the capacities you'd like to work on to improve your mental health. These affirmations are reminders of what you are capable of or are working toward. Rate each statement on a scale of 1 to 3.

1 = needs attention
2 = making progress or "good enough"
3 = this is a strength

SELF-REFLECTION AND INSIGHT

____ I'm capable of being aware of my current state of mind. I can mindfully notice what's going on without judgment.

____ I can generate insights and good guesses as to why I might be feeling, thinking, or acting as I am.

____ I can think things through and not be overly influenced by impulsive or automatic thoughts, stories, feelings, or urges.

____ I'm curious about my fluctuating states of mind and moods, and I try to be aware of the factors that influence my current mental and emotional state.

____ I'm able to be open-minded, reconsider my position, and broaden my perspective after taking in additional information.

OBSERVING YOUR MIND

____ I can observe what's going on in myself, and others, from a distance to prevent being hijacked by a racing mind or emotions.

____ I can simultaneously be having an experience and observe it with curiosity.

____ I notice and can make educated guesses about other people's states of mind and why they may be behaving the way they are, which informs my options for how to interact with others.

____ I'm capable of pausing before reacting to intense feelings or thoughts.

FOCUS AND ATTENTION

____ I'm willing to practice skills that give me greater control over my attention and racing mind, such as mindfulness, meditation, and breathing techniques.

____ I'm selective about the information I feed my mind, and I pay attention to the impact it has on my well-being.

GOOD JUDGMENT

____ I use good judgment and consider the consequences of my actions before deciding what to do.

STRATEGIZING, PLANNING, AND ORGANIZING

____ I use my mind to help me problem-solve and adapt to unexpected changes.

____ I organize and manage my time to provide helpful direction and structure to my days.

____ I make plans and work toward goals. I can direct myself with intention.

____ I'm able to tolerate the hard parts of being disciplined to achieve my goals.

____ I'm developing and using the amazing capacities of my mind to help me live well, and I can change or modify thinking that adds to my distress.

CHAPTER 6

Emotional Capacities

"Emotional intelligence is the capacity to recognize our own feelings and those of others, to manage emotions effectively within ourselves and in our relationship, and to use those emotions as a useful source of information and motivation."

—Daniel Goleman

Feelings enrich and inform our lives. Some emotions feel good and others are unsettling and painful. Some people see emotions as unnecessary, uncomfortable, unsafe, or not worth their trouble. They tend to suppress or disavow their feelings. Others feel too easily dysregulated by their emotions. In either scenario, emotions seem problematic. Instead, we want a healthy relationship with our emotions, which means being neither overwhelmed by nor detached from them. You can develop the capacity to identify and accept your emotions, tolerate feeling them, regulate them, and constructively process and use them.

> Make peace with your feelings.
> Let them enrich your life and inform you.

Feelings are natural, spontaneous responses to our experiences, and the type and intensity of emotions are influenced by our current *and* past experiences. Our initial physiological response to the activation of an emotion typically dissipates within 90 seconds.[1]

While we don't have much control over the initial emergence of emotions, we can influence their duration and intensity. For example, the way we talk to ourselves about our feelings has a powerful influence on whether the feeling passes, gets worked through, or becomes inflamed. Feelings are like the ocean: The waves come and go, and we can't stop them, but we can learn to surf.[2] We don't have to drown in them or stay out of the water for fear of them.

Avoiding emotions isn't a healthy strategy, because even when our minds try to ignore feelings, our bodies don't. Stress hormones are released in response to certain emotions, and that can lead to illness and other physical symptoms if we don't deal with the emotions constructively.

The easiest way to develop emotional capacities is to grow up in an environment where all your emotions are accepted as a natural part of being human, and your caregivers help you understand and regulate them. Initially, children need a lot of help managing feelings. They need caregivers to co-regulate: to name their feelings, tolerate them, help process them, and validate their experience. These children learn it's normal to feel upset or frustrated when their needs or desires aren't met, and to feel sad about losses. They'll slowly develop the capacity to regulate their emotions themselves.

However, many of us were raised by parents who didn't have healthy emotional capacities themselves. We may have learned that expressing certain feelings (such as anger, fear, sadness, or desire) got us criticized, punished, or shamed. Our caregivers' reactions teach us what is and isn't acceptable or safe to feel. Some of you were told to stop crying or acting like babies when you felt hurt or sad. If your caregivers can't tolerate certain feelings, you lose the ability to learn from and experience the full range of human emotions. The good news is that under improved conditions, you can have a better relationship with your emotional life and develop important emotional capacities.

Research shows people who are better at managing their emotions are less lonely and have better social relationships and improved cognitive functioning. They perform better at work and school, are physically healthier, engage in more positive behaviors, and are more satisfied with their lives.[3]

How to Facilitate a Healthy Relationship to Emotions

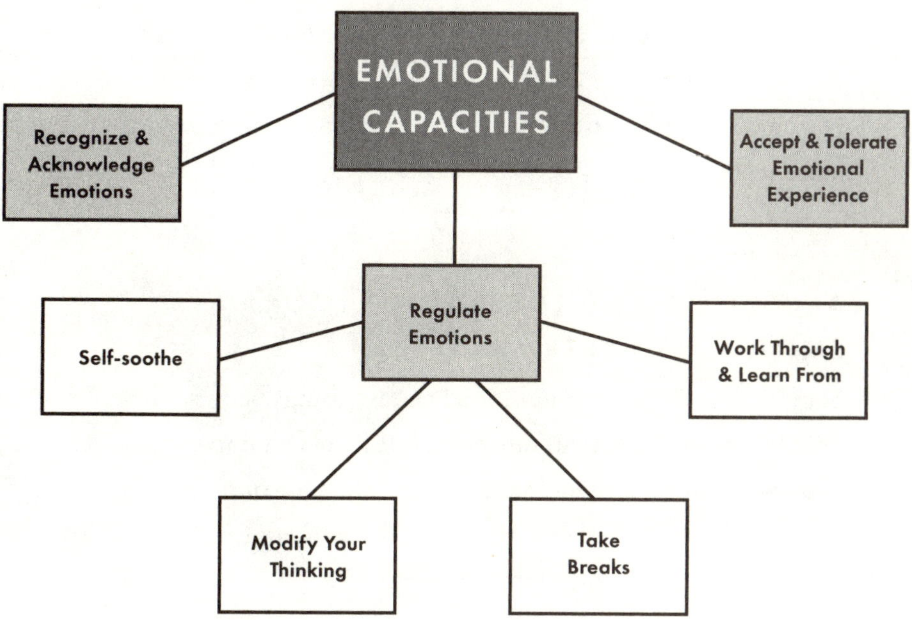

RECOGNIZING AND ACKNOWLEDGING YOUR EMOTIONS

The first step in facilitating a healthy relationship to your emotions is learning to recognize them. The six basic categories are: mad, sad, glad, afraid, surprised, and disgusted. Acknowledge your emotions with curiosity instead of judgment. While there is value in acknowledging your feelings, it's also important not to over-identify with them. You are not your feelings. You may feel sad or angry, but you aren't your sadness, and you aren't your anger. You're a normal human being having normal human experiences, which includes a lot of different emotions that come and go.

If you have a history of suppressing your feelings, you may have to learn how to identify them by paying attention to certain bodily sensations, such as flushed cheeks (anger or embarrassment) or a racing heart (anxiety). Certain thoughts can also clue you into what you're feeling, like "I can't believe he just did that!" (anger or surprise) or "I can't believe he's never coming back" (shock or sadness). Making the effort to name your feelings helps you shift your brain's activity from purely reacting and feeling to include a more reflective state.

ACCEPTING AND TOLERATING YOUR EMOTIONAL EXPERIENCE

Sometimes, we wish we didn't feel certain things because they hurt or make us feel bad about ourselves, but there's an important difference between tolerating emotions that spontaneously emerge and what we do with the feelings. As you'll see, there is value in being able to tolerate uncomfortable feelings.

Emotions happen for a reason, and we need to have the capacity to tolerate what we feel long enough for emotions to find healthy expression, to inform us, and for them to lead to insights and constructive actions. It's easier to make space for uncomfortable feelings if you can be empathic with yourself. Even if you're partially responsible for the way you're feeling, such as feeling guilty for hurting someone, try to appreciate that it's painful to work through difficult feelings, regardless of who caused them. There will be time to learn lessons from your emotions, but that's less likely to happen if you haven't become sturdy enough to tolerate them first. When you can accept and tolerate your feelings, you create opportunity to understand and constructively process them.

The inability to tolerate what we feel can lead to a variety of problems. We might recklessly act out our feelings without thinking of the consequences, or take our hurt or anger out on others, like yelling at your spouse or kids when you're mad at a friend or had a bad day at work. Feelings we can't tolerate also get channeled into our bodies, leading to physical symptoms. Some people avoid emotions by bingeing on substances or certain activities, which can lead to undesirable consequences.

Feelings won't kill us, but we often act as if they might. Tolerating emotions means we don't run away from or refuse to be present for our experience. It's true that some feelings can be excruciatingly uncomfortable, so it's understandable to need occasional breaks from them, pacing ourselves when we're feeling something big and consequential. If the situation activating the feeling is quite serious, the feelings are likely to be intense and thus will take more time and effort to work through. Be patient and kind to yourself as you expand your capacity to tolerate difficult emotions.

REGULATING YOUR EMOTIONS

There are four primary ways to regulate and constructively deal with your emotions: self-soothe, modify your thinking and attitude, take breaks, and work through your experience.

SELF-SOOTHING

Some emotions, such as grief, guilt, shame, anger, sadness, and fear, can be quite painful. Respond to your emotional state with sensitivity and care, as if you were dealing with someone who came to you with an injury. Try to empathically understand and appreciate, without judgment, your emotional experience.

Compassion takes this one step further and means you seek not only to understand but to help, to take some action to lessen the pain. You can comfort yourself with words or self-soothing behaviors. Try taking a hot bath or making yourself a cup of tea, sitting by the fire, wrapping yourself in a blanket or soft clothing, listening to music, lighting a candle, having your favorite meal for dinner, going out in nature, taking a walk, watching a show, meditating, taking a nap, reading, doing your favorite hobby, or talking to a trustworthy person. Exercise can also provide a healthy outlet for releasing emotional energy.

The tricky part with self-soothing is finding comforting activities that don't have additional negative side effects, like abusing substances or venting that turns into ruminating.

MODIFYING YOUR THINKING

What you think about your emotions and what you're going through has a significant impact on how you continue to feel. Certain kinds of thoughts and attitudes can make your original feelings either better or worse. When you catastrophize (exaggerate potential negative outcomes) and go down the rabbit hole of worst-case scenarios, it will likely add more suffering to your pain.

Imagine saying, "This is THE WORST thing ever! This ruins EVERYTHING!" You may *feel* that way but repeating the sentiment will likely intensify your suffering and interfere with constructive coping efforts. Repeating, "This is really awful *and*, somehow, I'll get through it one step at a time by tapping into my strength and courage," validates your feelings and calls forth your capacity to cope with whatever difficulties you face, however challenging.

The meaning you give the situation also matters. If someone breaks up with you and you tell yourself that it means you're not good enough and you'll never find someone to love you, your bad feelings will multiply. Instead, try to sit with the disappointment of your love or desire not being reciprocated and do not let it undermine your self-worth or rob you of hope in future possibilities.

There are numerous other unhelpful trains of thought or attitudes that can make our emotional lives more painful than they need to be (e.g., taking things too personally, overgeneralizing, all-or-nothing thinking). Become aware of how and when your thinking is harmful to your well-being and challenge it. When you're full of difficult emotions, seek input from your Wise Self, who can speak to you with a level head and be truthful, kind, and encouraging in the midst of your turmoil.

TAKING BREAKS

Sometimes emotions can be so intense, overwhelming, or complicated that it's necessary to take periodic breaks from them, especially if you're in a setting that isn't conducive for you to feel or express your feelings, like the office. While you don't want to avoid difficult emotions altogether, sometimes it's helpful to distract yourself temporarily. If you get too dysregulated (flooded with emotion), you're less able to access your rational mind and think clearly and constructively. You're more inclined to say or do things you later regret. In those moments, it's better to take a break or time-out to calm your nervous system.

Temporarily removing yourself from a heated situation and taking a few slow, long deep breaths can help calm your over-activated system down and prevent your emotions from escalating.[4,5] After the break, when you're more regulated, make sure to revisit what happened to learn whatever you need from that experience. Don't just sweep difficult matters under the rug or stuff your feelings into a vault once the intensity has died down. Remember, avoidance is not a successful long-term strategy.

WORKING THROUGH AND LEARNING FROM EMOTIONS

Investigate, make sense of, and process—that describes "working through." Meet your emotions with curiosity and courage. Be interested in what they represent and have to teach you, and be willing to work through whatever discomfort may be part of processing them.

Emotions call attention to what matters to us and has meaning for us. They also alert us to issues from the past that may still need attention. When you can make sense of something, you become better equipped to deal with it, rather than simply feeling at the mercy of it. Many of our current feelings are colored by past experience.

> When we don't work through painful emotions related to difficult experiences, those feelings tend to keep returning, seeking an outlet.

For example, sometimes depression is related to the unmourned losses that become a source of lingering, hidden sadness. In addition to actual losses of people or things that mattered to you, being disconnected from your authentic self can be experienced as a loss too. You may be chronically mourning repressed or disavowed aspects of yourself.

Freud introduced a concept called the "repetition compulsion," an unconscious drive to repeat past distressing experiences to achieve mastery over them in the present. When you haven't worked through traumatic experiences, they may get reenacted in the present. For example, if you had a parent who was alcoholic or verbally abusive, you may be drawn into relationships with alcoholic or aggressive partners. Unconsciously, you'd be hoping to achieve a better outcome, like helping that person get well and give you what you need this time around. On the other hand, you may be unconsciously reenacting old familiar ways of relating, fighting with, or rescuing others who need help as a way of feeling connected. If you have complicated relational dynamics like this in your history, a trained professional can help you better understand and work through them.

When old psychological injuries and the related emotions have been compassionately understood, tended to, and learned from, they typically cause less repetitive pain and disruption. Unresolved emotional issues can have an ongoing impact on your relationships, the way you feel about yourself and move through life, and your physical health.[6]

If you're not yet convinced that it's necessary or even valuable to feel your feelings, understand that when emotions are not processed (acknowledged, felt, expressed, worked through), they can get stored in or channeled through the body. Then, they show up in the form of physical discomforts such as headaches, digestive issues, neck/back pain, ulcers, sleep disturbances, and high blood pressure. Psychosomatic illnesses are physical conditions caused by or made worse by mental distress. These affect millions of people every year.[7]

Some people use defense mechanisms to deal with unprocessed emotions, such as smoking, overeating, or using other substances. Engaging in these activities will temporarily numb you out or distract you from your feelings, but avoidance has a physical cost. Remember that there are healthier ways to cope with emotions that don't cause you harm.

Coping with Anxiety

Anxiety, one of the most common feelings people struggle with, acts as a warning signal. It tells us that something threatening is happening or might occur, either in our external environment or within us, like the presence of conflicting or troubling thoughts, urges, or feelings. When real danger is imminent, our body responds to threats with an initial fight, flight (escape), fawn (appease), or freeze response. We get a shot of adrenaline and cortisol, which makes us alert and energetic enough to handle an emergency. Unfortunately, in the modern age, we tend to respond to too many things as if they are life-threatening situations.

For example, you may feel intensely anxious when you're facing things you deem intolerable, such as potential threats to your desires, self-esteem, or sense of control. And while those potential threats may feel scary and undesirable, life inevitably will include experiences that disrupt your sense of psychological security. That's why it's important to learn to address threats to your self-image, plans, and wishes in more constructive ways than panic and excessive worry. It also helps to figure out if the intensity of your anxiety is related to a past experience that hasn't been sufficiently worked through and needs deeper understanding and attention.

Many people have grown increasingly afraid of anxiety itself—as if the emotion were inherently bad. The goal of life is *not* to be free from all anxiety! If you care about things, you will feel anxiety. There is a lot going on in daily life that we can't control. Life often doesn't go according to our desires or the plans we so carefully lay out. It's normal to feel some anxiety when we're doing something that matters and we really want it to go well. Instead, make constructive use of anxiety.

Rather than despising or fearing your anxiety, see it as a normal human emotion signaling that you care about something or have a concern or worry that's calling for some attention. Use the anxiety signal to move into investigating your fear, discovering what's underneath it. Ask yourself

- What are you afraid of and why?
- How serious and likely is the threat?

- What, if anything, can you do to constructively address your fear or concern?
- How can you take care of yourself if you're dealing with something that doesn't look promising and cannot be changed?

Anxiety disorders can develop when your nervous system becomes overactive, hypersensitive to things that feel threatening, and your brain's threat-response system can get stuck on high alert. You may become hypervigilant, always on the lookout for danger. While it's understandable to feel distressed or afraid of being harmed or losing someone or something that matters deeply to you, you also need to be capable of accepting and dealing with the inevitable disappointments of life such as not getting promoted, losing a job, relationships coming to an end, and people we love dying or suffering from illnesses, accidents, and injuries. Life is full of uncertainty, and no matter how hard you try to control things, unwanted and unexpected events will happen.

Instead of accepting the uncomfortable reality of uncertainty, many people create an illusion of safety by convincing themselves they have more control over things than they do. They micromanage everything to create a sense of safety. Worrying can even be a form of control, because it can seem like you're actively doing something about your concern. But in fact, obsessively worrying rarely improves a situation. Worry is primarily useful when it draws our attention to a concern, and then activates compassion and constructive thinking and actions, or helps us process some of our feelings.

> Living in a constant state of stress, anxiety, or hypervigilance doesn't prevent life from unfolding as it will.

Responding with an outsized amount of anxiety or efforts to control the uncontrollable makes most things worse, not better. Thankfully we can develop and rely on more useful internal capacities to help us face anxiety-provoking, difficult, or unpredictable situations. We can meet our anxiety with compassionate curiosity and more useful methods of coping.

JOSEPH'S STORY

Joseph suffered from terrible anxiety and depression. When he was in college, his younger brother died of a drug overdose after taking OxyContin laced with fentanyl. The brothers went to the same university, and Joseph had been tasked by their parents with looking after his younger brother, who tended to be a risk taker.

Joseph's father blamed him for this tragedy. The father was ashamed and furious at his dead younger son for doing something so reckless. For a while, he forbade the family from even mentioning the deceased brother's name. Thus, Joseph's brother was not only dead but also exiled from the family's hearts and memories. The mother, meanwhile, spent considerable time in bed, simply surviving the devastating loss and wreckage that ensued.

Consequently, Joseph not only lost his brother, but he also temporarily lost his parents at a time when he needed them most. He had no "relational home"[8] in which to process the grief and guilt that haunted him. Furthermore, he felt pressure to make up for the loss of his brother and be a son his parents could be proud of. So, he lived cautiously, trying to never make mistakes, but that way of coping only heightened his anxiety and derailed his development.

Joseph lived with these unmourned losses, which left him depressed and highly anxious, for ten years before coming to see me. When he did, he was constantly on the lookout for what could possibly go wrong. After his brother's death, people around him seemed eager for him to move on or get over the loss. No one seemed able to tolerate his real feelings, which were often quite dark and painful. His parents had refused to get any grief or couples counseling, and they ended up divorcing. The tragedy of his brother's death was simply too much for a family that was already struggling with other difficulties, and now it seemed broken beyond repair. Joseph carried around unprocessed pain, and anxiety was a constant companion. At its worst, it came close to destroying his will to live.

It took time for us to work through all the elements contributing to his anxiety, depression, and suffering. Eventually, after courageous inner work, things improved. Joseph developed the inner resources he needed to heal and redirect his life. He finally had a safe place to talk about his brother, his only sibling, and express how much he missed him, how devastated he felt by that tragic loss and other losses. He learned healthy ways to comfort himself and cope with unsettling events and the disappointment of things not going the way he wanted. He discovered the courage to live in a world that is uncertain and, at times, even cruel.

Instead of living in a constant state of fear, Joseph redirected his energy into becoming someone who was capable and sturdy enough to deal with life as it unfolds. Rather than using worry and attempts to control life as his primary means of coping, he courageously and persistently experimented with new ways of approaching life that freed him from the prison anxiety had created. That challenging emotion became a source of information, rather than something stifling his life.

Change was an uncomfortable process for Joseph. Anxiety and rumination had become familiar company. But he learned to meet all of his emotions with greater compassion, curiosity, and constructive action. As he grew more comfortable with himself, he also turned down the dial on his fear of what others thought of him. An authentic sense of self emerged out of the shadows of who he thought he had to be. He practiced shifting his focus from the opinions of others toward reflecting on his own strengths and what he liked about himself, with enough space to accept his imperfections and quirkiness too. He grew to accept that in life, regardless of who you are, some people will like you and others will not—and he surprisingly found that he could live with that. He was determined to stop being a chameleon, changing according to what others wanted, as it had become utterly exhausting.

Joseph slowly learned to love himself unconditionally. He realized, "I am not my anxiety, and I am not my depression. My life will not be defined by my having 'failed' to keep my brother safe or my parents together. What happened was tragic, and I will miss my brother forever. But I am a unique, complicated guy with some good qualities too. I'm enough. I can deal with hard things." What a privilege it was to be on the journey of healing and self-discovery with Joseph.

Fear and worry are understandable emotions, but how you meet and process them is critical to your mental health. Joseph developed the emotional and mental capacities he needed to deal with anxiety and so much more. All that hard work awakened a deep-seated confidence that he could face life as it unfolds, instead of existing in a perpetual state of looking out for danger, worrying and catastrophizing, or trying to prevent unwanted experiences. His hard work awakened greater compassion, wisdom, agency, strength, and resilience.

EXERCISE: SELF-ASSESSMENT OF YOUR EMOTIONAL CAPACITIES

Use this self-assessment to identify the capacities you'd like to work on to improve your mental health. These affirmations are reminders of what you are capable of or are working toward. Rate each statement on a scale of 1 to 3.

1 = needs attention
2 = making progress or "good enough"
3 = this is a strength

RECOGNIZING AND ACKNOWLEDGING EMOTIONS

____ I appreciate the richness of my emotions and use them as one source of valuable information.

ACCEPTING AND TOLERATING YOUR EMOTIONAL EXPERIENCE

____ I can accept and tolerate my emotional experience however unpleasant it may be.

____ I willingly allow myself to feel the full range of human emotion, my spontaneous reactions to life events, without judgment.

____ I respond to emotions with curiosity and empathy and try to understand and appreciate why I feel the way I do.

REGULATING EMOTIONS

____ I have healthy ways of soothing myself when I am working through uncomfortable emotions.

____ I'm capable of challenging certain attitudes, thoughts, or stories I tell myself that exacerbate bad feelings and add unnecessary pain on top of legitimate pain.

____ I pace myself when dealing with uncomfortable emotions and take breaks from processing them as needed.

____ I courageously face and work through my feelings and the related issues they expose.

____ I respond to feelings with empathy and constructive action.

____ I use my emotions to understand myself and others better and can use that understanding to help me temper reactivity.

____ I investigate the meaning of my emotions to make sense of things.

____ I use my emotions to motivate me and teach me valuable lessons.

CHAPTER 7

Relational Capacities

"A good life is built with good relationships."

—Robert Waldinger

A comprehensive, longitudinal Harvard study set out to understand what makes people healthy and happy. Researchers discovered good-quality relationships were the most important predictor of who would enjoy happier, more fulfilling, and healthier lives.[1]

The spectrum of human relationships encompasses varying degrees of intimacy and closeness—from professional acquaintances and casual friends to close friends and intimate partners. Each relationship involves different degrees of involvement, boundaries, trust, and vulnerability.

To cultivate meaningful connections with others, we need to develop internal capacities that enable us to relate well to others. When you possess certain inner resources, you are better equipped to create and maintain good relationships and navigate the complexities of interpersonal life. Personal development enables you to be a more evolved and emotionally mature person, someone people appreciate and value being in a relationship with.

What Are Relational Capacities?

As we grow up, we learn how to relate to others from our caregivers and other people in our environment. "Implicit relational knowing" refers to the unconscious knowledge we possess about how to be in relationships. It's a form of *procedural* knowledge, which means knowing how to be or do something (in this case, relate) rather than *declarative* knowledge, which means knowing about something.[2] As a result, we develop unconscious ways of relating and expectations about how others will relate to us in various circumstances. We also develop a sense of what feels safe or dangerous about relating to others.

Implicit relational knowing develops through repeated relational experiences, and these patterns and ways of being in relationships become part of our autopilot. We unconsciously internalize the ways love and care was or wasn't shown—when love and support was given freely and unconditionally or only when you met certain expectations, or when "connecting" in your household included elements of conflict, aggression, control, or submission. We also witnessed and internalized relational patterns related to handling conflict. Did family members discuss and work through their inevitable differences, or did they blow up, insist on their points of view, withdraw, or avoid conflict altogether? What relational patterns and expectations became part of your autopilot?

Most of us internalize at least some unconscious ways of relating that don't serve us well as adults. We all grew up in imperfect interpersonal contexts with other imperfect human beings, and you'll want to become aware of the unhelpful relational tendencies you learned so you can modify them through insight and new experience. You need opportunities to participate in new and improved ways of relating with others so you can replace your less helpful autopilot tendencies with healthier, more satisfying ways of relating. It helps tremendously if these new opportunities are with people who already have the capacity for healthy relating or are motivated to learn better ways of relating with you.

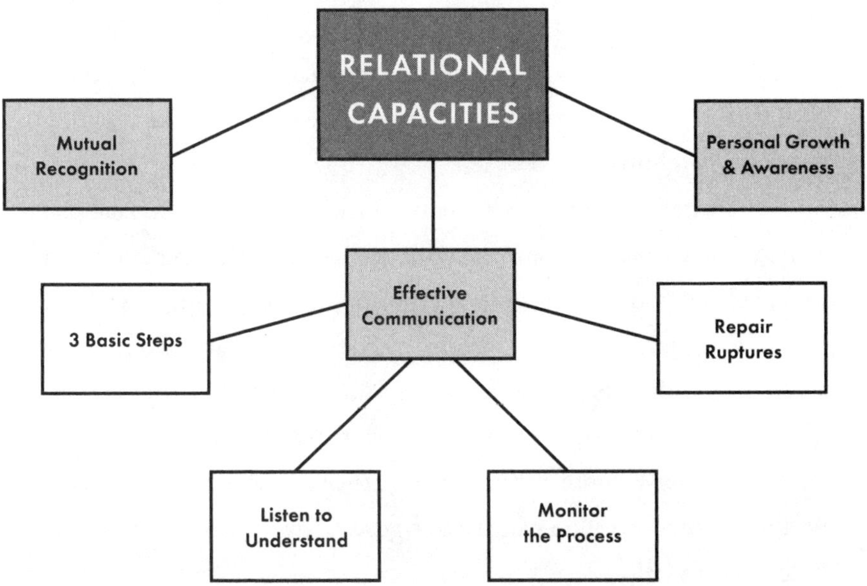

Personal Growth and Awareness

Self-awareness includes the ability to notice and understand your emotions, thoughts, physiological states, strengths, and shortcomings, as well as your autopilot tendencies, intentions, values, and impact on others. Insight helps you better understand why you behave as you do and improves your ability to make conscious choices and change. Self-awareness and insight contribute to personal growth and emotional maturity, which is characterized by a more sophisticated understanding and management of your emotional world, coupled with the capacity for empathy, cognitive flexibility, personal agency, and resilience.

Emotionally mature individuals do well in relationships because they tend to be more emotionally stable, flexible, trustworthy, and reliable.[3,4] They are open to others' perspectives and boundaries, show appreciation, and are authentic and appropriately vulnerable, which deepens trust and connection.[5,6,7] It's easy to see how all these qualities would make anyone a better friend, co-worker, family member, neighbor, and partner.

Self-awareness and insight help you observe your internal life honestly and make sense of your experience, including how you are relating with others—what you might be feeling, needing, wanting, or intending. You notice the stories you're telling yourself about your experience, both helpful and unhelpful narratives. When you're aware of the factors contributing to your current experience, you have more influence over them. If you're not relating well with someone, you can try to figure out why and what adjustments might help.

The highest level of awareness also includes the capacity to understand and take into consideration other people's states of mind as you interact with them. Are they in a bad mood because their dog is sick, or they only slept a few hours last night, or they have a big test or project due today? Some couples find it useful to make a habit of keeping each other informed if they're having a tough day or are in a difficult mood. That communication helps your partner not take your current mood personally and gives them an opportunity to be more patient.

AWARENESS OF UNHELPFUL STRATEGIES PEOPLE USE TO INFLUENCE OTHERS

Try to become more aware of tactics you use to influence others to get what you want and need, because some tactics hurt your relationships.

One of my patients learned that by guilt-tripping her mom, she could get what she wanted. Her mom worked long hours and felt guilty for not being more available and missing important events. When my patient really wanted something, she would find a way to remind her mom of this "failure." In response, her mom would become extra generous or permissive to assuage her guilt. My patient found herself unconsciously repeating this pattern with her husband, which drove him crazy: "Can't you negotiate for what you want from me without trying to make me feel like I'm not enough?!"

Aggressive or manipulative methods to get attention or influence others erode trust and goodwill. Examples include guilt-tripping; excessively criticizing, negating, or discounting the other person's experience; stonewalling (withdrawing or withholding); and threatening, controlling, or being demanding. When you use tactics that evoke shame, fear, or guilt, the relationship suffers. Even if they work in the short term, in the long term they usually alienate others.

That said, behaving passively and abandoning your own needs is not an effective strategy either, as it breeds frustration and resentment. Self-awareness allows you to notice behavior that could be unintentionally harming your relationships. Motivation to learn more effective methods of influence that address your needs *and* preserve the relationship begins with awareness.

ADVOCATING FOR YOURSELF

You need to be aware of what matters to you and feel worthy enough to make sure your needs and desires are considered. Growing up, you may have learned that it wasn't safe or didn't work so well to advocate for yourself. But if you want satisfying relationships now, you must find the courage to speak up on your behalf. Don't expect others to read your mind; simply hoping people who care about you will know what you want or need isn't a good strategy and places an unfair burden on them. Accept responsibility and communicate what you desire.

Instead of being passive or aggressive, be assertive in your interpersonal relationships, advocate for yourself, and express your preferences. You can share your needs while also appreciating the reality that others may have competing desires that also deserve consideration. Being assertive doesn't guarantee you get what you want, but it improves the odds.

Self-awareness improves your ability to relate well with others. It empowers you to see what's going on during interpersonal interactions and make adjustments as needed. When you understand your desires and tendencies, you can use those insights to grow and mature into someone more capable of forming and maintaining healthy relationships. Ultimately, the more aware and insightful each person in a relationship is, and the more willing they are to work on their own personal growth and emotional maturity, the better.

Mutual Recognition

We all have a need to feel recognized by others. Mutual recognition is the capacity to see each person in the relationship as having a separate, equally important mind of their own with a distinct center of feeling and perception. If there is only room for one person in the relationship to be seen, heard, and understood, you won't be able to create a mutually satisfying relationship. Everyone has their own subjective way of experiencing things. We are not clones of each other. Even though we sometimes wish others saw things the way we did, life is more complicated than that. To forge healthy relationships, both parties need to have mutual respect for each other's rights, boundaries, differences, and autonomy.[8,9]

> One of the more challenging aspects of close relationships is how to work out the inevitable clashes of desire and perspective that will emerge from two uniquely different human beings.

Moments when you each want something different can feel frustrating and challenging. Giving up something you desire as part of a compromise can be hard, sometimes really hard. You'll have to figure out equitable ways of reaching compromise, which include adequate space to prioritize each person's hopes and desires some of the time.

When you blend two worlds together, you need to be able to recognize and deal with the uniqueness of each person. Then you can thoughtfully navigate differences and even turn them into opportunities for personal growth and enrichment.

EMPATHY

Understanding the importance of mutual recognition helps you better appreciate the vital role empathy plays in relationships. Empathy is the act of trying to imagine and appreciate another person's subjective experience. You can still be empathic even when you wish the other person felt or saw things differently and don't fully agree with their perspective. Start by making an effort to understand their personal and unique experience, instead of arguing over who is "right" or "wrong." Remember that each person is influenced by their own attitudes, beliefs, expectations, and history—the truth of their experience.

Healthy relating is enhanced by the capacity to show empathy and recognize each person's reality, feelings, and desires. Here is a suggestion for developing more empathy in your relationships:

- Ask: "Why or in what ways does this issue matter to you?"
- Listen with the intent to understand, without prematurely negotiating, debating, or interrupting to insert your perspective or "fix" anything.

Empathy helps you constructively address the issues creating tension between you. Until each person's unique perspective is heard and understood, it's harder to make much progress on resolving issues in a mutually satisfying way. Even though you won't always be on the same page, you can still try to be on the same team, caring about what's good for each of you and the relationship.

Effective Communication

Research overwhelmingly confirms that good communication is foundational for healthy and fulfilling relationships, whether romantic, friend, or familial.[10] It acts as the bedrock upon which understanding, trust, and connection are built. We learn about others when they communicate their thoughts, feelings, desires, wishes, and concerns. We teach others how we want to be treated by what we communicate. Without effective communication, relationships are more prone to misunderstandings, hurt feelings, conflict, resentments, and eventual breakdown. Mutual self-disclosure and vulnerability is one way to learn important things about each other, and it can build intimacy and strengthen bonds.

Good communicators express their desires and concerns in ways that improve the likelihood they'll be heard. Unfortunately, many of us communicate our feelings and wishes in a way that provokes defensiveness in the other person. And it's pretty easy to evoke another person's defensive urge to argue with us or shut down, when what we really want is to invite curiosity in what we have to say and a willingness to sort through the issues at hand with us.

> Strive to be honest and non-aggressive with your communication.

Imagine you start off a conversation with a harsh tone of voice, emphasizing how wrong or disappointing the other person is. Most people feel a powerful instinct to protect themselves from what they perceive as an attack—your criticism. The attacked person's energy goes into litigating the complaint, presenting their counter point of view, making excuses, or explaining how your experience is wrong and they're not the bad person you're making them out to be. If they have healthy self-esteem, they'll be less likely to be defensive because they can accept that they're imperfect and behave poorly sometimes. They are open to feedback. They can acknowledge fault and know that they'll sometimes disappoint others without those disappointments erasing their other good qualities.

Unfortunately, you can't magically give someone else healthy self-esteem, but you can present your complaints in a way that evokes less defensiveness. If you want to be heard, don't come in guns blazing. Yelling and criticizing may get their attention, but doing so typically activates tendencies to protect and defend rather than listen and consider. Bring up your concerns and offer feedback without harshness—be as kind, calm, and clear as you can. How you present your concerns has a significant impact on how the conversation unfolds.

THREE BASIC STEPS FOR EFFECTIVE COMMUNICATION[11]

1. Describe what's upsetting you: "When __________ happened, or you said __________."

2. Share how you're feeling: "I felt/feel ______________ (sad, disappointed, angry, confused, afraid)."
3. Make a request for change; say what you want or need:
   a. "Please don't yell at me, or be so harsh, or ________."
   b. "Next time please ask me nicely, or apologize, or ________."

Keep your comments focused more on how you feel and ideas for repairing things and encouraging better behavior in the future, rather than primarily focusing on your complaint and their disappointing behavior.

When someone hurts you, it can evoke a primal urge to retaliate. Resisting the instinct to strike back requires emotional maturity and impulse control. A more mature, effective, and growth-oriented response is to share your experience and request better treatment. If you have been treated poorly, consider the following general communication skills as a constructive alternative to retaliation:

Focus on the person's behavior and avoid attacking their character. Talk about what the other person has said or done, or isn't saying or doing, that is bothering you. Character assassination and harsh criticisms such as, "You are the most selfish person I've ever met," "You *never* do anything nice for me," or "How could you be so stupid?" not only evoke defensiveness, but they also make people feel bad about themselves, which isn't the most effective way to draw out better behavior from them. Furthermore, it can escalate the conflict and invite counter attacks.

Be specific in letting them know how you've been impacted by what they did, and what you want instead. Try to convey some belief in their ability to do better. Speak to the part of them that seems most capable of changing, rather than reinforcing feelings of being inadequate or incapable. Use assertiveness and encouragement, not harshness and shame.

If the other person does show some remorse and understanding of why you are upset, accept their apology. Try not to keep dwelling on their wrongdoing, as this will likely reawaken their defensiveness. Remember, the objective is to have the offending person understand your hurt, disappointment, and concerns and be motivated to do better next time. Reinforce any efforts they do make to improve the situation or their behavior.

LISTEN TO UNDERSTAND

It can be difficult to hear someone is unhappy with or disappointed in you, but if you've done or said something that bothers somebody, it's helpful to communicate to them that you understand their feelings and the impact you had—even if you hadn't intended to upset them. Do your best to listen to what they have to say.

Afterward, let them know what you heard. For instance, "You want me to know that you don't like it when I make sarcastic comments," or "You want me to understand that you felt unimportant when I didn't include you in the plans." This is called active listening, and it invites reciprocity and constructive dialogue. Then you can take your turn to describe your perspective and experience. People want to feel seen, heard, and understood: Once they see you're trying to understand them, they're much more likely to reciprocate and listen to your perspective.

Listening and offering empathy in this way doesn't necessarily mean you agree with their interpretation of events. It simply means you acknowledge their point of view and feelings. If you've both listened to each other with the intent to understand, it'll then be easier for you to move on or work through the problem and negotiate a compromise between your differing needs and desires.

MONITOR THE PROCESS

Be aware when a conversation gets overheated and the way you're talking to each other is no longer helping you work through the issue. It helps if both people have the capacity to regulate their emotions before and during difficult conversations and are willing to admit when they've said or done something hurtful. However, we're all human. There will be times when one of you is so dysregulated that the way you're expressing yourself is making things worse. A time-out may be needed.[12] Either person can stop and say, "This conversation is clearly not going so well right now. Can we pause, take a minute, and start over?" Or "Talking this way to each other is making things worse. We can do better. Let's try again."

It's important to calm your nervous system before restarting the conversation. Take deep breaths, go outside for a walk, or do something else to discharge negative energy and shift your mindset. After you've sufficiently soothed and regulated yourself, try again using the three steps outlined previously: Describe what happened to upset you, say how it made you feel, and tell the other person what you need to help repair things now or in the future.

When you're upset, you may feel the urge to vent. And sometimes it feels cathartic to express yourself freely without having to censor what you say. Yet, while some venting might seem helpful, you may need to vent to someone who isn't the person you're upset with. Or perhaps you can learn to vent without being mean or hostile or inflaming the situation so the person you're upset with can tolerate a little venting. But keep in mind that simply discharging your emotions doesn't typically resolve issues, and it can make things worse if you remain focused on the most negative aspects of the situation or person you're upset with.

REPAIR RUPTURES

Everyone is capable of behaving poorly. You won't always be at your best. People make mistakes and do or say things they regret. Some issues evoke such strong reactions and feelings that our capacity to talk about it in a constructive manner is temporarily compromised. You might raise your voice to emphasize your point. A little extra volume may not always derail a conversation, but saying mean things is unhelpful and injurious.

Rupture and repair is a normal part of all relationships. Be humble enough to admit when you've behaved poorly or hurt someone, even if you didn't intend to hurt them. You could say, "My bad, I shouldn't have said or done that. That was unnecessary and hurtful." A simple but sincere "I'm sorry" can go a long way to repair things and restore trust.

When you do something hurtful, attempt to repair the situation as soon as possible. Some people avoid dealing with their "misdeeds," hoping that time will either lessen the negative feelings or the other person will forget what they said or did. But the truth is, most people will remember what happened, unless the offense was minor. Clear the air and reset the tone between you. You don't want to accumulate too many unprocessed grievances that can leave ugly scarring. Repair attempts that include empathy and apologies restore a sense of good will and cooperation.

General Tips for Effective Communication

- **Use the three basic steps of effective communication:**
  - Describe what's bothering or concerning you
  - Say how you feel about the situation
  - Ask for what you need to make things better, now or in the future
- **Speak your truth non-aggressively.** Your tone and delivery make a difference in how well your message will be received.
- **Focus more attention on what you need or prefer**, and less on your complaint and criticisms.
- **Listen nondefensively, with the intent to understand** the other person, even if you see things differently.
- **Communicate an understanding of the other person's perspective.** Let them know what you heard.
- **Monitor the process.** Regroup and restart conversations that are getting too negative. Take a break when needed.
- **Repair with empathy and apologies** when you say or do something hurtful, even if it was unintentional.

> No matter your upbringing, you can become someone who is capable of communicating in ways that make it more likely that others will listen.

Working through upsetting situations often requires a combination of understanding, empathy, humility, forgiveness, patience, and a willingness to regroup and redirect when things are moving in an unhelpful direction. Arguments usually represent important conversations that need to happen, but how you communicate will make a significant difference in how well that conversation goes. Some people avoid difficult conversations for fear of it going poorly, but avoidance usually leaves you feeling distant or resentful. You want to co-create enough safety in the relationship for each of you to feel seen and known, to be open and honest, and to trust that with the right kind of effort and good communication, you can work through hard issues together.

Impact of Positive and Negative Interactions on Your Relationships

Research on marital satisfaction gives us some important data to hold in mind when thinking about important relational capacities. The ways you interact create a certain energy between you, and that energy impacts your feelings for each other, your state of mind, your nervous system, and the overall quality of the relationship.

We communicate with words, tone of voice, body language, and behavior. Most interactions can be considered positive, neutral, or negative. Research shows that couples with the most satisfying marriages have an average ratio of 5:1 positive-to-negative interactions.[13]

When this ratio dips toward equal amounts of positive and negative interactions, or the negatives outweigh the positives, the marriage is much more likely to experience distress and there is a higher likelihood of divorce.

Positive interactions include a nicer tone of voice, kind gestures, pleasurable touch, humor, appreciation, affirmations, patience, understanding, empathy, and encouragement. Examples include saying thank you, giving a hug or kiss or gift, showing admiration, giving compliments, being helpful or performing acts of service, listening attentively, sharing a laugh, engaging in shared interests, showing affection, and spending time together. These positive interactions create and preserve a sense of good will between you.

I ask couples to respond to the prompt: "I feel loved and cared about when you ___________________." They each create a list of ten specific things that make them feel loved and cared about and share it with the other.[14] This exercise helps your partner be more aware of your personal "love language," ensuring they know how to show love in ways that truly register for you.[15]

Negative interactions can feel harsh or destabilizing, and they can provoke fighting and hostility. They include irritability, impatience, rudeness, meanness, criticism, defensiveness, and withholding. Such interactions can leave you feeling frustrated, disregarded, unseen, hurt, angry, unsafe, dysregulated, or unappreciated. We're only human, so there'll be times when we may be unpleasant or negative. Try to make sure those moments are vastly outweighed by more positive, skillful ways of interacting.

Learning to interact in constructive and positive ways, while keeping negativity to a minimum, greatly impacts the quality of your relationships. Cultivating good communication capacities and skills helps you to build more satisfying connections, navigate interpersonal challenges with greater success, and experience deeper fulfillment from your interpersonal life.

JORDAN AND ALMA'S STORY

When Jordan and Alma came for couples therapy, they were on the brink of divorce. They were both quite unhappy in their relationship, vacillating between patterns of silence and withdrawal or combat.

Jordan was raised to be a tough, competitive man. His father was a ruthless businessman who pitted Jordan and his two brothers against each other in constant competition to see who was the best. He believed this would toughen up the kids and force them to excel. They were taught to never admit fault, as it might imply weakness. Winning and succeeding at any cost were the driving family values. Family members connected through arguing, debating, and competing with each other.

Alma was raised by a father who provided well for his family and expected submission to his authority in return. Her mother was a quiet, conflict-avoidant, people-pleasing woman, who suffered along without complaint, rarely expressing her wishes. Alma got the idea that being loved meant being taken care of and "managed," and showing love meant you should accommodate others' desires and expectations while suppressing your own.

Given Jordan and Alma's backgrounds, they initially seemed to fit well together. Jordan was a successful businessman and the authority in the home. He provided well for their family. Alma played her part by being an accommodating wife, always attentive to the needs of others. But while the qualities Jordan's father had encouraged in his youth—competition, aggressiveness, a drive to triumph over others—helped him get ahead in business, they didn't enhance his relationships.

The impetus for change began when Alma realized that she could no longer ignore how unsatisfied and unhappy she felt in the marriage. She embarked on a journey of personal exploration and growth, awakening many suppressed desires. She wanted to be treated like an equal and express herself more freely. She longed for a relationship where love was expressed with kindness and affirmations, where she could share her desires and needs without being lectured or dismissed.

Jordan was unsettled by these changes in his wife. He didn't understand why the "old way" had stopped working. He loved Alma and didn't want a divorce, so he agreed to try couples counseling. He admitted he had no idea how to relate to Alma in any other way, but he was willing to try.

As Alma took the risk to more freely share her desires, displeasures, or differences of opinion, Jordan reflexively rolled up his sleeves and set out to win every debate. He had a hard time taking off his high-powered-lawyer hat. He eventually realized it was more important to save his marriage than win yet another argument with his wife. I suggested he think of their disagreements or differences of opinion as needing mediation rather than a trial.

At the beginning, empathy, mutual recognition, non-defensive listening, and making repairs were foreign concepts to both Jordan and Alma, but they were willing to try out new ways of relating to each other. We learned more about their autopilot ways of relating and began working on the ones causing the most harm—including lack of awareness, being overly controlling, not listening to understand, difficulty respecting each other's unique subjective experience, aggressive communication (or none at all), unwillingness to admit fault or apologize, self-sacrifice to the point of resentment, and withholding as punishment.

Their communication improved and Jordan and Alma began making efforts to infuse more positive interactions into their daily lives, like offering compliments, helping each other with projects, taking walks together, starting and ending their days with a hug or kiss, going on fun outings, listening to music or watching shows together, and so on. They tried debriefing about their days while they ate dinner each night, sharing the highs and lows they'd experienced that day, rather than looking at their phones or watching TV. This became a meaningful way of connecting at the end of the day.

Alma worked on having more agency and asserting herself in the relationship. Previously, she'd held her emotions in, building up resentment and hurt feelings until she couldn't stand it any longer. Then she would lash out. She learned how to talk about her concerns in ways that invited understanding and compromise, and Jordan slowly learned to listen without arguing. They learned to tolerate the times they disappointed each other and came to understand and grieve some of the more disappointing aspects of how they were raised. They got better at accepting feedback and delivering it with less harshness.

The benefits of making these changes were reinforcing for the couple. The more they embodied new ways of relating, the deeper the connection between them grew—a major improvement over domination and self-negation.

As Jordan changed, his friendships and work relationships began improving as well. Greater awareness led him to observe the ways his upbringing had hardened him and hampered the development of more insightful and caring parts of himself. He began to feel some relief at not always having to win or be right. In the past, people respected his intelligence and worldly success but didn't feel especially safe or at ease with him. Now, the efforts he made to be a better communicator and more empathic improved not only his marriage but other relationships too.

Relational capacities of self-awareness, mutual recognition, and good communication take time to develop. Personal growth and maturity are an ever-evolving process. You can become a better communicator. You can learn to align your actions with values and choices that enhance good relationships and build trust, respect, and affection. These capacities help you build and maintain good relationships. Keep developing the capacities you need to have conversations and interactions that better meet your relational needs and desires and lead to greater fulfillment.

EXERCISE: SELF-ASSESSMENT OF YOUR RELATIONAL CAPACITIES

Use this self-assessment to identify the capacities you'd like to work on for personal growth and to improve your mental health. These affirmations are reminders of what you are capable of or are working toward. Rate each statement on a scale of 1 to 3.

1 = needs attention
2 = making progress or "good enough"
3 = this is a strength

AWARENESS AND INSIGHT

____ I know myself well enough to recognize my needs and preferences so I can advocate for them.

____ I'm aware of my particular sensitivities, tendencies, and protective strategies that can interfere with healthy relating, and I'm willing to work on them.

____ I'm learning to use healthier ways of getting my needs met and am willing to modify aversive methods I learned to influence others.

____ I'm using self-awareness and insight to help me mature into someone capable of building and maintaining good relationships (e.g., someone trustworthy, insightful, appreciative, and respectful).

MUTUAL RECOGNITION

____ I recognize and respect that others have a separate and equally important mind of their own with a distinct center of feeling and perception.

____ I aim to be empathic and strive to understand other people's experience and point of view, even when it's different from my own.

____ I work toward addressing differences in a way that both people feel understood and taken into consideration.

____ I strive to work through differences and reach compromises both parties can live with, instead of trying to win arguments or insisting on getting my way.

____ I'm equally comfortable with my sense of separateness and autonomy as I am with closeness and intimacy.

EFFECTIVE COMMUNICATION

____ I communicate in ways that increase the likelihood of my message being heard and are less likely to evoke a defensive response.

____ I listen non-defensively with the intent to really understand the other person's experience.

____ I'm honest and direct with others, and I say what I need to say as kindly as possible.

____ I can describe what upsets me, share how it makes me feel, and make a positive request for change that could improve the moment or situation.

____ I make an effort to repair things and make amends when I contribute to misunderstandings, hurt feelings, or other interpersonal difficulties.

____ I focus my feedback on the behavior that hurts or concerns me, rather than attacking someone's character.

____ I suggest "time-outs" when a conversation is getting more negative or unproductive. I can request that we reset and try again.

CHAPTER 8

Healthy Coping Strategies

"In the midst of winter, I found there was within me an invincible summer . . . It says that no matter how hard the world pushes against me, within me there's something stronger, something better, pushing right back."

—Albert Camus

People generally want to feel good, feel safe, and avoid pain. Yet pain is unavoidable. Every person's life will include a mixture of joys and sorrows. We'll be presented with challenges on a regular basis. As much as we might wish life could be good all the time, it won't be—hard to accept, but true.

Thankfully, we can develop inner resources to help us face challenging realities and feelings. In fact, research shows that the quality of our lives is greatly impacted by our ability to cope with adversity and find healthy ways to get our needs met. When we use healthy coping strategies instead of relying on unconstructive methods or avoiding what's difficult, we have greater success navigating life and become more resilient.[1,2,3,4,5]

How Healthy Coping Strategies Develop

Developing healthy ways of coping is easier said than done for a variety of reasons. For starters, to cope well you need essential inner resources you may not have developed yet. Other factors can interfere, as well. For instance, if you grew up in an environment that included significant trauma, abuse, poverty, or neglect, you were forced into survival mode. Coping meant doing whatever you had to do to get by. That kind of coping is usually scrappy and necessary but not highly sophisticated and skillful.

Facing serious difficulties growing up can also impact the development of your brain structures. Your fear-response system may become overactive. Childhood trauma can alter the functioning of the prefrontal cortex, the part of the brain crucial for executive functioning—emotion regulation, decision-making, planning, and impulse control.[6] If your caregivers are overwhelmed by their own difficulties, they'll have a harder time helping you develop yourself enough to cope effectively.

Since no one was raised in a flawless environment, there's a good chance some of your old coping tendencies from childhood aren't serving you well as an adult. Some people may also have biological conditions that make it harder to use their minds effectively. Don't be too hard on yourself if this is the case. You did the best you could at the time, given your circumstances, and there are still ways you can improve your coping mechanisms.

Self-Protective Strategies

Before we discuss healthy coping strategies, it's important to understand how our desire to protect ourselves can interfere with our ability to effectively handle challenges. As I said earlier, humans go to great lengths to avoid pain. The problem is that many methods of avoiding pain create other problems, and we refer to those methods as maladaptive or unhealthy coping strategies.

We all develop self-protective mechanisms early in life, psychological defenses that serve to ward off unpleasant or overwhelming thoughts and feelings. The more difficult your growing-up environment was, the more energy you had to expend to protect yourself from painful and fearful experiences. The end result is that kids dealing with unhealthy environments are more likely to submit to, fight against, or not trust others as ways to protect themselves. Defenses and self-protective strategies become part of your autopilot.

> We all need ways to protect ourselves from being overwhelmed by pain or threatening experiences.

Psychological defenses aren't uniformly bad. Yet problems occur when we over rely on defenses and develop unhealthy coping strategies that interfere with learning more effective ways to deal with hard things.

Here are some commonly used self-protective measures that can cause other problems.

AVOIDANCE STRATEGIES

To protect yourself from potential discomfort or disappointment, or the exertion required to do hard things, you avoid what burdens, scares, or threatens you. For example, you don't try new activities if you might fail. You don't have hard conversations. You don't let yourself pursue goals that might be difficult to achieve.

These are examples of avoidance strategies:

- **Procrastination:** You put off or avoid doing what is anxiety provoking or difficult to do. You tell yourself, "I'll do it later," as if it somehow will be easier to do tomorrow. Performing unpleasant tasks rarely becomes more inviting later. A fair number of tasks we need to accomplish to succeed in life involve pushing through resistance and getting it done.
- **Repression:** You unconsciously block out distressing memories, thoughts, or emotions to protect yourself from the uncomfortable or bad feelings that come from facing them. People who were molested tend to repress those memories as they feel unbearable to think about. If you did something you're ashamed of, you might repress that memory to avoid feeling guilt or shame.
- **Apathetic withdrawal:** You protect yourself from being hurt, rejected, or disappointed by becoming indifferent and detached. You avoid doing things that might subject you to evaluation for fear of criticism or failure. You convince yourself you don't care so the outcome won't affect you as much. But when you stop caring, you cut yourself off from your interests, hopes, and ambitions.

CONTROL TACTICS

You exert tremendous effort to control your environment, yourself, and others to prevent unwanted things from happening. This gives you *a sense* of greater protection from uncertainty, an illusion of being able to prevent pain or disappointment. The truth is, of course, that while we have the ability to influence life, our ability to control it is limited.

Control tactics manifest in many ways:

- **Obsessive-compulsive tendencies:** You exert control over tangible objects to give you a sense of control over your body, impulses, and physical environment, and to protect yourself from chaos and anxiety. Behaviors such as triple checking that doors are locked, endlessly tidying your home, or obsessively monitoring what you eat can give you the illusion that you're protecting yourself from some potential danger, from being out of control, or from allowing something bad to happen. These behaviors give you a *sense* of predictability and safety.
- **Controlling others:** You expend a great deal of energy trying to make other people behave in ways that make you feel better or more secure, to protect yourself from the pain or fear of being disappointed or hurt by them, or to avoid seeing them make mistakes or get hurt.
- **Controlling outcomes:** You exert excessive effort attempting to make life go the way you want it to, often to the point of behaving without integrity. You do this to protect yourself from being disappointed or feeling like a failure. Cheating is one way people try to get what they want and prevent an unwanted result.
- **Omnipotence:** You convince yourself that you have more power or control than you do to avoid feeling helpless, weak, fallible, vulnerable, or anxious. For example, you may tell yourself and

others that you're brilliant and you never make mistakes so they'll think highly of you. You get to feel good about yourself, and they feel protected or inspired by your supposed brilliance. The illusion feels reassuring.

DENIAL

You deny, disavow, rationalize, or suppress what you can't bear to know, face, or feel.

Denial can show up in different forms:

- **Rationalization:** You make up plausible justifications for unacceptable behaviors, thoughts, or feelings. This involves explaining away your or other people's actions in a seemingly logical or socially acceptable way to avoid facing the truth or consequences of your actions or decisions. You rationalize to protect your self-esteem and reduce anxiety. For example, you might say, "I lied to my friend because the truth would've hurt her too much," when in reality the truth would've made you look bad. Or "Sure, I cheated a little on the test (or game or application), but so does everyone else. You need to do it to stay competitive."
- **Dissociation:** You temporarily disconnect or detach from unbearable, overwhelming, or intolerable experiences. This is a form of being cut off from oneself and acts to protect you from overwhelming stress or trauma. Individuals facing inescapable threats like rape or other violence often survive by "checking out" so they don't experience the horror in real time.
- **Disavowal:** You reject or expel from consciousness anything you find unacceptable about yourself, others, or your circumstances

to protect yourself from the anxiety and pain that would come from facing it.

MORE EXTREME OR AGGRESSIVE MEASURES

You aggressively go after what you need or feel entitled to in order to protect yourself from feeling shortchanged, denied, or left out. Or you use extreme thinking to protect yourself from something you don't want to face or feel.

- **Blaming others:** You externalize responsibility for all that's bad or wrong with life onto others by excessively criticizing, complaining about, blaming, or devaluing others. This protects you from feeling responsible, inadequate, remorseful, or guilty.
- **Projection:** You see in others the unacceptable qualities you refuse to see yourself capable of, such as lack of integrity or aggression. You project the "badness" onto others because, consciously or unconsciously, you can't bear to admit that these aspects do or could also reside in you or people you think highly of.
- **Devaluing, idealizing, splitting, and black-and-white thinking:** Black-and-white thinking or splitting means you divide people or things into "all good" or "all bad" to keep it simple and avoid more complex realities. It can be hard to accept that good people, especially people we count on, like our parents or leaders, can do really bad things. Splitting is a way to avoid the discomfort of ambiguity and uncertainty. You may also devalue others in order to feel better about yourself in comparison. You give simplistic explanations for problems, finding "villains" to blame. You decide problems are being caused by "the other," "those troublemakers," and not "us good people."

Idealization means attributing exaggerated positive qualities to yourself or others, and it is used to manage anxiety and protect your self-esteem. Seeing yourself or others as perfect or all-powerful protects you from the reality that people have flaws, will disappoint us, and don't have all the answers. Some people tend to feel safer in the hands of an all-good or all-knowing savior-type person. People with this coping strategy are vulnerable to charismatic cult leaders.

> When you learn to tolerate the truth of your experience, including painful emotions and realities, you won't need to use defense mechanisms as often.

Defense mechanisms can provide a protective function when we're most vulnerable, but relying on them excessively creates problems because it hinders our abilities to engage with reality, build healthy relationships, experience a full range of emotions, and develop more mature and adaptive coping strategies. Defense mechanisms also use up a lot of mental energy and play a role in self-destructive behaviors, such as when the use of denial or rationalization keeps us from seeking help for addictions or other harmful behaviors.

Essential Ingredients of Healthy Coping Strategies

Instead of avoiding difficulties with unhealthy strategies such as running away from challenges, denying reality, acting out your pain, numbing out, or being overly defensive, you can develop yourself into a more aware, insightful, thoughtful, persevering, and courageous problem solver. Instead of slapping quick-fix bandages over your problems or difficulties, you can develop inner resources that enable you to accept and tolerate the inevitable discomfort of real life and its challenges, regulate your emotions and impulses, and make wiser decisions.

Healthy coping strategies give you a chance to thrive, rather than merely survive or live in a cocoon created from limiting self-protective strategies and defense mechanisms. Let's dive into the ingredients of healthy coping.

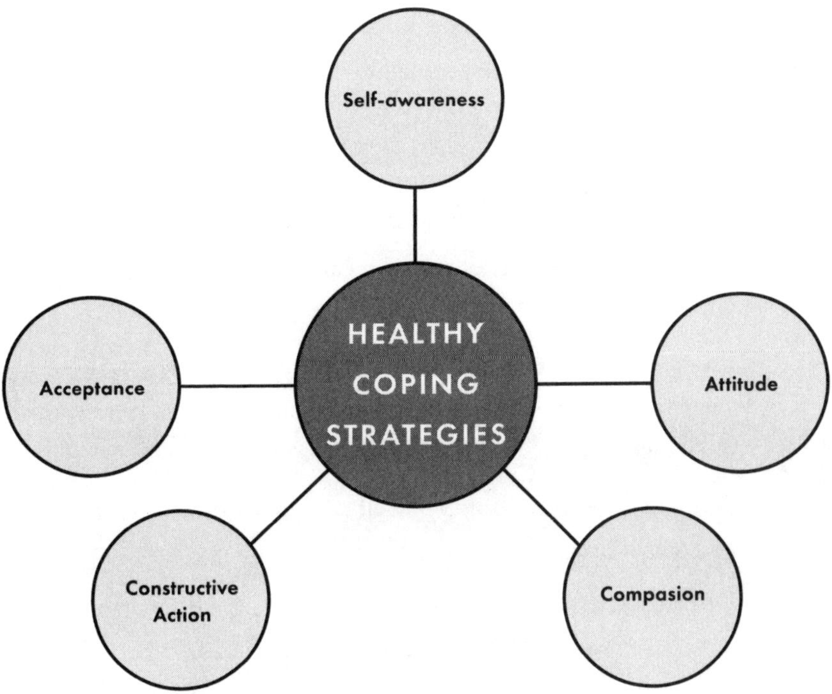

SELF-AWARENESS

Self-awareness allows you to recognize your autopilot tendencies for coping and protecting yourself. You can't change what you're not aware of. Looking back on your life experience, try to understand how you protected yourself from the difficult parts of growing up in your environment. Explore the following questions:

- How did you cope with the hardships you lived with, such as pain, fear, and uncertainty?
- Did you learn it was better to avoid conflict to avoid inflaming others?
- Did you cope by denying painful realities, or making excuses for the people hurting you so they wouldn't seem like "bad" people?
- Did you learn it was easier to suppress your needs and desires than risk hoping for something and being disappointed?
- Did you find comfort or safety in carefully controlling whatever you could?
- Did you find that complaining was the most useful release valve for your frustrations, and safer than the risk of trying to change things?
- Did you disconnect from yourself and your experience to avoid feeling pain?
- Did you learn to be helpless because efforts to effect change or be assertive might have felt too risky or futile?
- Did you learn to aggressively protect yourself and take what you needed out of fear that nothing short of that would work?

We all have ways of protecting ourselves and getting our needs met that we may not like or be proud of. Remember that we developed those strategies for a reason. Ask yourself honestly which of the strategies you rely on are worth keeping. Figure out which ones are effective and help you live a good life, and which ones no longer serve you well. Have compassion for yourself as someone who was doing the best they could, especially when you were young. But now you have a chance to re-evaluate and modify your coping strategies, to develop more constructive ways to deal with your pain and difficulties. Change starts with awareness.

ACCEPTANCE

Two kinds of acceptance help us cope effectively in life: the ability to face reality as it is, and the ability to accept that things won't always go our way. Fighting against reality or remaining overly attached to expectations adds to our suffering. It's important to learn to accept life as it unfolds and not put our heads in the sand. Bargaining with or demanding that life go according to our hopes and plans rarely works. It's hard to accept the losses or hardships we encounter, but fighting against or distracting ourselves from painful realities that need to be faced and worked through is not a good use of our valuable energy.

You can't successfully address an issue if you refuse to accept that it's an issue. Even worse, addictions can develop if you over rely on behaviors like drinking, drug use, overeating, overworking, compulsive shopping, scrolling, gaming, or gambling to cope or avoid reality.

> Equanimity is a superpower, the ability to stay calm and steady while accepting whatever reality you face. "For now, this is what is."

The serenity prayer reminds us to accept the things we cannot change, change the things we can, and be wise enough to know the difference. It captures a critical aspect of effective coping. We learn to accept life as it is and develop the capacity to tolerate and work through the disappointments and pain that are an inevitable part of the journey. Once we accept reality, we can mourn our losses and look for ways to constructively deal with them, however undesirable, knowing we can find a way through our difficulties.

COMPASSION AND SELF-CARE

You can't change the fact that hard things will happen, but you have control over how you treat yourself in the process. Dealing with challenges can be painful. Offer yourself the same compassion and kindness you would to someone you love and care about who is facing a difficulty. If you feel guilty about something you've done that contributed to the problem, you can be compassionate with yourself for the pain you're in *and also* reflect on why you behaved poorly, commit to doing better next time, and consider making amends. Compassion doesn't mean we let ourselves off the hook when we have something to learn and realign.

But during a crisis, when you're hurting and upset, good self-care helps you stay calm, steady, and strong while you figure out your options for handling the troubling situation. Get some rest. Try to minimize the use of coping strategies that could also harm you, like overindulging in comforting activities that make you feel worse later. Do something you find soothing or that gives you a needed break from the intensity of the pain, like exercising or listening to music, taking slow deep breaths to calm your nervous system, or talking to a supportive person. Be a safe harbor for yourself when you're hurting and weathering something painful.

ATTITUDE

The attitude we bring to every situation critically impacts how things unfold, how we feel, and how effectively we cope. When difficulty strikes, we can learn to respond with attitudes that reflect courage and hope:

- *"I can deal with hard things."*
- *"I can find my way through this incredibly difficult situation."*
- *"This is really brutal, and I refuse to let it take me down."*

If you faced horrible circumstances at a young age, this kind of confidence may not have been possible. Instead, you may have developed an attitude of defeatism, hopelessness, helplessness, or rebellion. Thankfully, as you grow older, you have a chance to develop your inner Warrior Self, the part of you that is or can be strong and determined, that is no longer a victim of circumstances, and that reflects growing confidence in yourself.

You can adopt an attitude wherein you think of failures or hard times as teachable moments—opportunities for you to learn and grow stronger. You can learn to guard against catastrophic thinking or ruminating on the worst-case scenarios. While it's understandable that your mind may gravitate toward worst-case possibilities in the face of the unknown, you don't want to let yourself get stuck there.

Strive for a balanced perspective and hopeful attitude. Psychiatrist and Holocaust survivor Victor Frankl reminds us that "everything can be taken from a man but one thing: the last of the human freedoms—to choose one's attitude in any given set of circumstances."[7] Trust that you can deal with whatever hard things are happening. Maintain self-talk that is realistic, strong, comforting, and supportive. Don't minimize the seriousness of your circumstances, but embody an attitude of believing in yourself and your determination to keep facing what's in front of you with as much strength and courage as you can muster—one moment and one step at a time, to the best of your ability.

CONSTRUCTIVE ACTION

When dealing with a crisis or difficulty, ask yourself these two questions:

- *"Is there anything I can do right now that can keep things from getting worse or that might improve things?"*
- *"How can I take good care of myself while I navigate this challenging situation?"*

Sometimes there's no concrete action that can be taken to effect change in the way we most desire. If your loved one was just diagnosed with a terminal illness, for example, that is devastating news and you can't really make that better. However, you can be compassionate with yourself given the pain and anxiety you're feeling. You can offer love, help, and support to your loved one. You can call a supportive person and let others help you. You can pray. You can let yourself have a good cry to release some of your pain and sadness. You can take deep breaths to calm your nervous system. These are constructive actions.

Do your best to direct your attention and energy into constructively helping yourself weather the bad news or distressing turn of events. If you can't change the situation, you can at least talk yourself through the difficulty with compassion and wisdom. Try not to make matters worse by endlessly spiraling out on *would'ves, should'ves*, and *what ifs*. Do your best not to layer any extra suffering on top of the legitimate pain you're already in.

The more we develop our inner resources, the more capable we become of constructively dealing with challenges with some degree of equanimity. This means remaining grounded and steady in the midst of turbulence. Crises are the time you most want to be able to rely on clear thinking, good decision-making, and emotion regulation. While understandable, freaking out doesn't do much to help you address your difficulty. Be patient with the process of finding appropriate solutions to problems and resist the urge to turn to quick fixes, or reactive, less effective ways of coping. Patience and steadiness are psychological muscles that need to be exercised to grow. Author Anne Lamott says, "It's good to do uncomfortable things. It's weight training for life."[8]

> You develop resilience by courageously working through life's challenges and setbacks, changing circumstances, stressful situations, and losses.

As you practice coping with challenges in life, you become more resilient—the ability to bounce back from and successfully deal with adversity—a capacity that develops through facing and navigating difficulties. We are not born with it and you can't buy it. As we're first learning how to cope, we initially look to others to help us and we borrow from their strengths. Eventually, we develop our own capacities to stay steady in the face of challenges—using our minds and good attitudes to help us tend to our pain and do what makes things better, not worse. We become resilient.

Summary of Necessary Ingredients for Effective Coping

1. **Awareness:** Know yourself well enough to be aware of your coping habits—how you tend to respond to crises or difficulties. Try to catch yourself if you're engaging in old, unhelpful ways of coping.
2. **Acceptance:** Acknowledge reality and deal with it rather than fighting against, denying, or avoiding it. Accept what isn't under your control.
3. **Compassion:** Have empathy for what you're experiencing. Be kind to yourself as you navigate the difficulty you're living through.
4. **Attitude:** Stay grounded in the belief that you can and will be able to deal with the difficulty you're facing, however painful it might be. Challenge self-talk and beliefs that are defeatist and erode the sense of hope and determination you need to tap into.
5. **Constructive Action:** Whenever possible, see if there's anything you can do to improve the situation and take better care of yourself in the process.

When we bring awareness, acceptance, compassion, helpful attitudes, and constructive action to each challenge we face, we become more resilient and strengthen our capacity to cope effectively. The Wise, Loving, and Warrior parts of yourself can help guide you through difficulties. You'll need all your inner resources to successfully navigate tough times in ways that do not diminish your life. Healthy coping is captured well by an attitude of believing in your capacity to deal with whatever challenges you encounter.

When Life Tested My Coping Capabilities

Tuesday, September 30, 2014, started out as a fairly ordinary day. After my morning walk and shower, I left for a busy day seeing patients. Around 2:00 p.m., a sweet text message from my 27-year-old son brought a smile to my face: "I love you so much mother, always, always." I knew Wiley was in the midst of a busy day too, one that included picking up keys to his new Brooklyn apartment, prepping for English classes he was teaching to college freshmen, and organizing friends to help him move. An hour later, a call from the New York Police Department destroyed my ordinary day. The luxury of living under the illusion that life is relatively safe and predictable came to a screeching halt. I was catapulted, kicking and screaming, into a world I no longer recognized or knew how to be in. Twenty-four hours later, I found myself peering through a dirty glass window at the morgue, identifying my son, whose body was covered by a flimsy pink plastic sheet.

Wiley's death shattered me—my way of being in the world, my sense of self, and a future I had taken for granted. I became an alien in a world I no longer could relate to: regular people having everyday experiences—laughing and smiling or dealing with minor disappointments and stress. People who could wake up with some assuredness that their loved ones would choose life over death that day. All I wanted was impossible—to wake up from a wretched nightmare, to rewind time, for Wiley to be alive and healthy. And I dreamed repeatedly of encountering Wiley, alive in my dreams, which left me overcome with gratitude and relief, followed by a wave of embarrassment that we'd now have to tell everyone his death was all a big, horrible mistake. Instead, I woke up once again to my unbearable reality, an unimaginable present, and a future without Wiley in it.

It took everything in me to keep putting one foot in front of the other. I was shattered. Heartbroken. I wasn't sure how I'd survive the pain of such a devastating loss, but I didn't want my only other child, Elise, to suffer the loss of both her only sibling and her mother due to inconsolable grief. That motivated me to dig deep and find a way to navigate the hardest thing I've ever faced in life.

The process wasn't pretty or graceful. On the contrary, it was agonizingly difficult to come to terms with my horrible and unwanted new reality. Life as I knew it changed in an instant, and I had no power to undo what was. After a period of merely surviving the devastation, I had to dig deep for healthy coping strategies. I couldn't afford to add any additional pain to the legitimate agony I was experiencing.

During that dreadful time of grief and suffering, I learned what it meant to take exquisitely good care of myself. I learned to be compassionate and patient with myself in a way I'd never known until then. I said "no" more often, stopped being hard on myself, and took naps every day. I let the love and kindness of others help me through, something for which I'll be forever grateful.

My grief left me feeling broken and fragile—just crushed—which was quite a change from my previously driven and energetic way of moving through life. The tears and grief seemed endless. I had to accept life was certainly not going according to my plans, and there were vital things I couldn't control or prevent despite enormous effort. I didn't want this to be true.

Slowly, oh so slowly, I learned to deal with my new reality. I found ways to emerge from my heartbroken hole back into the land of the living. Today, I'm a more resilient, courageous, patient, and compassionate person because of what I've been through. My belief that I can deal with hard things was tested beyond what I thought I could endure. I am grateful I survived the worst of it and kept looking for ways to cope that would not result in me living as a shell of my former self. I'm not the same, but I'm not diminished either. I've been molded into someone different, someone who has a wider container for the sorrows and joys life includes. I discovered a strength hidden within me I didn't know I possessed.

I want you, too, to find and create within yourself the capacities you'll need to navigate this wild and unpredictable ride we're on called life. And my heart goes out to you for the pain and suffering you've had to or will face in your lifetime. No matter what has been, no matter what may come, have faith in yourself and your growing capacities to navigate what at first glance may seem impossible or too much to bear.

EXERCISE: SELF-ASSESSMENT OF YOUR COPING STRATEGIES

Use this self-assessment to identify the capacities you'd like to work on for personal growth and to improve your mental health. These affirmations are reminders of what you are capable of or are working toward. Rate each statement on a scale of 1 to 3.

1 = needs attention
2 = making progress or "good enough"
3 = this is a strength

SELF-AWARENESS

____ I'm aware of the difference between the healthy and unhealthy ways I try to protect myself from threatening or unpleasant experiences.

____ I make an effort to understand my automatic reactions and tendencies when upset or faced with a difficulty.

____ I notice when I'm starting to cope in unconstructive ways and make an effort to modify my approach.

ACCEPTANCE

____ I accept the realities of life.

____ I willingly and wisely accept the things I can't change or control.

____ I don't waste too much energy insisting that life be different than it is. I deal with what is.

COMPASSION AND SELF-CARE

____ I acknowledge the difficulty and pain I'm in, and I offer myself compassion while I work through challenging experiences.

____ I take care of myself while in a distressed state so I can find the energy required to cope effectively with difficulties.

ATTITUDE

____ I believe in and strengthen my capacity to work through hard things.

____ I praise myself for and foster all efforts to constructively handle challenges.

____ I redirect overly negative thought loops and catastrophic thinking.

____ I challenge defeatist attitudes that interfere with a sense of hope, possibility, and determination.

CONSTRUCTIVE ACTION

____ I effectively cope with difficulties by taking constructive actions that help improve the moment or situation.

____ I talk to myself with compassion and encouragement when facing something difficult, as I would talk to a good friend.

____ I avoid or redirect actions that might make the situation worse.

____ I stay solution-oriented when facing difficulties, using my energy for useful purposes such as self-soothing and problem-solving.

____ I turn to my inner Warrior Self to find the strength I need to face challenges.

____ I remember that I'm much more than my problems, and that my resilience grows with each hard thing I face and work through.

CHAPTER 9

Your Journey of Personal Growth and Development

"And the day came when the risk to remain tight in a bud was more painful than the risk it took to blossom."

—Anaïs Nin

How do we develop the capacities we lack in order to create a stronger foundation for good mental health and a fulfilling life? How do we heal psychological wounds and untether ourselves from self-defeating thoughts, behaviors, and tendencies? And how do we cultivate constructive coping strategies and healthy ways to meet our needs for pleasure, safety, recognition, connection, agency, and purpose?

Fortunately, personal growth and change are possible. Unfortunately, it's not always easy. It takes time and courage to understand your internal landscape and address what's limiting your life. Meaningful change requires both insight and new experience.

Instead of over relying on quick fixes to feel happy or avoid pain, invest time and effort into developing yourself. It will be a rewarding, and at times challenging, journey. So, be patient, persevering, and kind to yourself as you begin this process of self-discovery, healing, and growth.

Don't be discouraged by setbacks. Change is typically challenging in direct proportion to

- How deeply ingrained your more troubling tendencies are
- How developmentally depriving or harmful your growing-up environment was
- How much neglect, abandonment, emotional enmeshment, abuse, loss, or trauma you experienced and may need to work through
- The severity of biological deficits that could be making things more challenging for you, from genetics, illnesses, and disabilities to difficult life experiences that negatively impacted the development or functioning of important brain structures
- Difficulties accessing internal or external encouragement and resources that would support your efforts toward healing and personal transformation

Remember that your unhealthy behaviors and symptoms exist for a reason. They have or had some meaning or purpose, originated out of a need, and reflect how you attempted to meet that need or adapt to your circumstances. It takes time and repeated efforts to reprogram ingrained ways of being and operating, behaviors, and attitudes that got wired in over years or even decades. If you're used to protecting yourself and getting your needs met in certain ways, it won't be easy to relinquish these tendencies, which you formed for understandable reasons. You can grow quite comfortable with familiar patterns, even if they limit your life. Change can feel scary. In other words, expect some parts of you to resist changing.

Deeper psychological work typically requires assistance. It helps to have a new welcoming and safe environment that is accepting and encouraging of your explorations, healing, and development. It's enormously beneficial to have someone healthy, wise, and well-informed to learn from and work with as you're exploring and expanding yourself. Trustworthy guides are insightful and affirming of your authentic self. They aim to help you become a wise and caring advisor to yourself.

My greatest hope for you is that you become a person with a healthy sense of self and the capacities to form meaningful relationships, make good use of your mind and emotions, and wisely navigate the harder parts of life.

Let's take a look at what is involved in this journey and what kind of help is available.

Facilitating Growth and Change with Insight and New Experience

INSIGHT

One common ingredient across all five inner resources is self-awareness. When you do the work to better understand yourself and your experiences, you gain insights. However, expect some internal conflict between the part of you that sees the value in becoming more insightful and a part that might not be as interested in deeper exploration.

Self-exploration and honesty open the doors for new discoveries and possibilities. Yet it can be hard to see that you may have a lot of inner work to do. It can be painful to honestly revisit and work through experiences in your life that injured you and led to unhealthy coping, but growth begins with learning to be aware of and honest with ourselves. Change involves developing curiosity about our autopilot rather than just letting it blindly run our lives.

When you better understand yourself and others by gaining insight, you're less likely to be overpowered by your thoughts, feelings, urges, and memories. Awareness and curiosity lead to reflection and insights. You learn to check in on yourself, asking, "What's going on right now? Why am I feeling this way? I wonder why I (or they) are behaving that way? How accurate or helpful is the story I'm telling myself right now?"

Based on your history, certain situations will activate intense emotions. From a place of greater knowing, you come to understand your tendencies. As a result, you feel less confused by your reactions. When you are having a strong reaction to something, you can practice pausing to make room for awareness and insight, which leads to better, more informed responses.

When you understand how you came to be the way you are, you tend to be more compassionate with yourself for the less helpful ways of being you developed growing up. You can be kinder to yourself as you courageously face and work on ungrieved losses, injustices, disappointments, anxious or avoidant attachment patterns, insecurities or shame, and unhelpful coping strategies.

Awareness and insight are invaluable; yet they don't always feel good. Try not to let that stop you from being honest with yourself. Developing the capacity to face, feel, learn from, and bear the realities of your life sets you on the path to greater freedom and possibilities.

NEW EXPERIENCE

Knowledge and insight alone are typically not enough: We also need new experiences to facilitate meaningful change and transformation. Those new experiences need to be cultivated and reinforced to become strong enough to override the old autopilot ways of being that constrict your life.

It takes courage and a willingness to experiment with thinking and behaving in new ways—to relate to ourselves, others, and the world a little differently—with more awareness, wisdom, flexibility, and expansiveness. Repetition and experimentation will be necessary to modify your autopilot. As new experiences get wired into your operating system, they can compete with and eventually override old, less helpful tendencies.

Don't let yourself be discouraged too easily. The process of growth and change is typically uneven, with lots of ups and downs. At times, you'll get derailed by old patterns. Your job is to keep bravely and thoughtfully exposing yourself to greater understanding and new learning opportunities. When the outcome is not as positive as you'd hoped, don't give up. No one on earth instantly and gracefully transforms into a new, more evolved version of themself. The journey can be long, messy, and, at times, scary, but it's worth the effort.

Some people have just enough inner resources and determination to make changes without professional assistance. However, most of us benefit from having a trained professional help us begin and stay the course, to warmly embrace our whole self, and to encourage the development of all we're capable of.

Good therapy gives you an experience of being deeply seen, understood, respected, and believed in. Remember that children internalize the experiences they have growing up and that becomes part of their autopilot—how they unconsciously operate in relationships, cope, and how they think of themselves. Therapists co-create new experiences with you that can be internalized too. How you interact with your therapist is part of the process of developing important psychological capacities and a healthier sense of self. Therapy offers you the opportunity to be in a relationship where you're encouraged to be honest and curious, to express and tolerate all feelings, to take risks and learn from mistakes, to be assertive, to use your mind to gain insight, to form connections, to courageously face difficulties, to develop healthy coping mechanisms, and to become your fullest, most authentic self. It can be invaluable to have a trustworthy person guiding that process, someone devoted to prioritizing your needs and growth with you.

What Kind of Help Is Available?

People are motivated to seek help for a wide variety of reasons, with varying needs and goals. It helps to know what you need to work on before searching for a provider. For example, you may want to improve your relationships or self-esteem, live with more agency, navigate a particularly challenging crisis, work through unresolved issues, modify unhelpful coping mechanisms, or address more serious mental health conditions. Depending on what you need help with, there are different types of assistance available.

Seek out a well-qualified person to help you with your particular needs. You want someone knowledgeable, insightful, and empathic helping you face the truth of your experience, which can include intense emotions. Psychic pain becomes more bearable when it can be named, thought about, felt, made sense of, and shared with a trustworthy person. Take a few sessions to see what it's like to open up to them. Ask yourself:

- Do I have a good feeling about them?
- Am I comfortable with their manner and approach?
- Do they have sufficient training and experience given my needs?
- Do they ask questions that encourage me to think deeply, feel freely, and explore things of importance?
- Are they responsive and engaged?
- Do they welcome my full uncensored self, all parts of me?
- Do I feel understood and respected by them?
- Do they work collaboratively with me and is our work together helpful?

Get referrals from trusted sources whenever possible. Websites like *Psychology Today* can help you learn about and find therapists. Be selective and find someone who seems like a good fit.

Most people who seek therapy have a positive outcome.[1] If you don't feel like your treatment is going well, bring that up with your provider. Be honest and forthcoming with concerns you may be having about your work together. If they're not receptive to your concerns, or the two of you can't satisfactorily adjust the way you're working together, then you may need to find someone else with a different approach or manner. You deserve the opportunity to have a good collaborative relationship with someone who can help you better understand yourself, heal, and evolve.

Different Types of Therapy

As the number of people seeking mental health support increases, more individuals are engaging in therapy—not only for relief from psychic pain or an acute crisis but also as a meaningful path toward personal transformation. For decades, people have consulted doctors to care for and improve their physical health, personal trainers to keep their bodies strong, and spiritual teachers to nurture their spirituality. Finally, there's less stigma associated with seeking help with your mental and emotional well-being as well. In fact, these days it's often considered admirable and wise to make that investment in order to keep learning and evolving.

There are many different approaches to therapy and change, and each approach places greater emphasis on what they think is the cause of people's suffering and difficulties, and what will be most helpful to focus on for treatment. Some therapists use multiple modalities and modify their approach depending on what they believe each patient needs most. People sometimes try more than one type of therapy as they figure out what's most helpful for them given their current and evolving needs.

There are three primary ways therapists try to facilitate change. **Behavioral therapies** are rooted in the principles of learning theory, and they focus primarily on changing behavior using techniques such as exposure therapy, systematic desensitization, reinforcement, and behavioral activation to help you unlearn certain behaviors and learn new ones. **Cognitive behavioral therapists** place greater emphasis on identifying, understanding, and changing *thoughts and beliefs* that contribute to emotional distress and problematic behaviors. **Psychodynamic therapists** tend to put greater emphasis on having a holistic understanding of multiple factors that influence a person's sense of self and ways of operating, including how *unconscious processes* and past experience influence present-day thoughts, feelings, and behaviors.

PSYCHODYNAMIC PSYCHOTHERAPY

Psychodynamic psychotherapy explores hidden, unconscious motivations and patterns that contribute to current difficulties. It recognizes the impact of your childhood experiences and past relationships on your development, helping you understand your autopilot—how you came to be who you are and why you have the tendencies you have. It uncovers the reasons for, history behind, and meaning of your experience.

Therapist and client co-create a facilitating environment for the patient's self-discovery and continued development, forging a deep and trusting relationship. This enables you to safely experiment with new ways to open up, process emotions and traumatic memories, see and think about things more expansively, and modify the way you engage with and navigate life.

This kind of deep exploration typically takes time, and the duration of treatment can vary greatly. In some cases, it's beneficial to meet more frequently than once a week, especially if you have a history of trauma or are working through material that requires more containment and support.

COGNITIVE BEHAVIORAL THERAPY (CBT)

CBT focuses on helping you identify, challenge, and change unhelpful thinking patterns and behaviors that contribute to your distress. Negative or unhelpful thought patterns and cognitive distortions, such as, "I'm a loser," "I can't change," "If I don't get this job, I'll never succeed," and "No one will ever like me," are believed to be primary causes of negative emotions and behavior. CBT teaches practical strategies to change unhelpful or self-defeating thoughts and beliefs that are contributing to your difficulties.

CBT is typically a more time-limited, structured approach than psychodynamic psychotherapy, as it focuses more on the impact of your thought patterns and present-day problems rather than diving into the past. That said, newer forms of CBT are expanding to include mindfulness and compassion practices, as well as deeper exploration of the origins of thoughts and beliefs, and greater attention to emotional processing.

OTHER SPECIALIZED THERAPIES

Here are some examples of specialized types of therapy, each one offering a particular focus and approach.

- Mindfulness Based Therapy (MBT) anchors treatment around the importance of learning to be mindfully aware and is loosely based on Eastern meditative practices.
- Acceptance and Commitment Therapy (ACT) helps you accept difficult thoughts and emotions and commit to actions aligned with your personal values in order to create a meaningful life.[2]
- Internal Family Systems (IFS) strives to help you understand and heal the multiple internal parts of yourself, and develop greater self-compassion, harmony, and a wise leader or "CEO" of your internal family system.[3]
- Inpatient care is available for when you need a more contained setting for treatment of issues such as drug or alcohol rehabilitation, certain eating disorders, or when you're in crisis and need 24-hour supervised care.
- Psychoanalysis is an intensive form of outpatient therapy intended for in-depth exploration of your unconscious dynamics and typically involves multiple sessions per week.
- Dialectic Behavior Therapy (DBT) was created primarily to treat borderline personality disorder (but is sometimes included in the treatment of eating disorders and other addictions or mental health conditions), using the following skills-training components: emotion regulation, distress tolerance, interpersonal effectiveness, and mindfulness.[4]

PSYCHOTROPIC MEDICATIONS AND BRAIN-STIMULATION TREATMENTS

Biological-based interventions are also available. Psychotropic medications, such as antidepressants, are prescribed by medical doctors to impact neurotransmitter levels or receptors in the brain that affect mood and cognitive functioning.

Even though medications can help address biological issues contributing to your difficulties, they don't "fix" everything or give you good mental health. If you're taking psychotropic medications, I encourage you to also make use of additional resources to help you improve your mental health.

For more serious mental health conditions that aren't responsive to less invasive forms of treatment, transcranial magnetic stimulation (TMS), which uses magnets to stimulate brain cells, and electroconvulsive therapy (ECT), which uses electrical currents, are options. These treatments directly target and modify brain activity that affects certain mental health conditions. Neurofeedback is another method used to help people self-regulate brain activity and has been used to treat attention-deficit hyperactivity disorder (ADHD).

Alternative Resources

Beyond formal therapy, there are many other resources and self-help materials available to support your mental health and wellness journey. These range from life coaching, communal support groups, and educational materials like books and podcasts, to experiential opportunities such as workshops and retreats. (See the Appendix for book recommendations and additional resources.)

LIFE COACHING, WELLNESS RETREATS, BOOKS, AND PODCASTS

Life coaching isn't the same as therapy, but it's a resource for people interested in receiving help with a specific goal, overcoming obstacles, and creating actionable plans to enhance their personal or professional lives. Its focus is more on the present and future. It's largely an unregulated profession, as anyone can call themselves a coach, so make sure to ask about the person's training, experience, and any certification they've received.

Wellness retreats can give you time and space to nurture yourself and your well-being. The mind and body are interconnected, and diet and exercise also have a significant impact on your mood and energy. Avail yourself of whatever resources help you take good care of all aspects of your health.

Reading books and listening to podcasts can prove inspirational and informative, but don't be surprised if you also need some professional help on your journey toward better mental health. Do your best to match your chosen resources with your specific needs.

TEXTING SUPPORT, MENTAL HEALTH APPS, AND FRIENDS

Most healthcare practitioners aren't readily available for spur-of-the-moment sessions, so additional resources can be helpful when crises erupt or when you're struggling in between sessions and wish you had someone to talk to right then. Your provider may be able to schedule extra phone sessions or appointments some of the time, but otherwise it's good to have additional options.

Crisis Text Line provides immediate, confidential mental health support via text messaging 24/7. Text "home" to 741741 to begin getting text support. You can also dial 988 to speak to a trained crisis counselor for urgent mental health needs. If you're having a mental health emergency, you can also go to the nearest hospital emergency room.

There are mental health apps offering additional support, such as guided meditations, breathing exercises for anxiety reduction, sleep support, mood tracking, and thought challenging tools. But your mental health and well-being deserve good quality care and attention, so don't limit yourself to apps if you need something more. I prefer to think of apps as one tool you can use to support your overall efforts to take better care of your mental health.

In addition to professional help, it's so helpful to have other supportive and trustworthy people in your life you can turn to in times of need, people you feel safe being honest and vulnerable with. They can't fix your pain or problems, but they can offer empathy and understanding that helps you feel less alone.

> A precious gift we can give to each other is to hold space for listening and caring in times of need.

If someone in need calls you for support, ask if they are looking for a sounding board and empathy, or if they want your advice and ideas on how to deal with their predicament. Would they prefer your kindness and good listening or concrete help? Most of the time, people in pain first and foremost simply want to be heard. I recommend starting with empathy and listening and then ask if they would also like to hear your perspectives, suggestions, or opinions.

SPIRITUAL PRACTICES

Spirituality holds significant value for many people due to its multifaceted benefits, which touch upon various aspects of human experience. For starters, it can help provide a sense of purpose and meaning in life and believing in a source of power greater than oneself can also provide comfort, strength, and support during difficult times. Spiritual or religious groups also connect you to a community of like-minded people who share similar values and beliefs.

Studies show that spirituality can have positive effects on mental and physical health, and increase feelings of peace, joy, and well-being.[5] Religions and spiritual teachers generally promote positive qualities such as compassion, forgiveness, and gratitude, and encourage practices such as meditation, prayer, and self-reflection. Spiritual practices can provide a sense of grounding, purpose, and connection that can help you lead a values-driven life.

ALTERNATIVE TREATMENTS BEING EVALUATED

Research on psychedelic-assisted therapies is experiencing a tremendous resurgence, with promising results emerging for some mental health conditions.[6] Studies are investigating the efficacy of substances such as psilocybin and MDMA in treating post-traumatic stress disorder (PTSD), anxiety, addiction, and depression.

MDMA is a synthetic drug that acts as a stimulant and mild

psychotic, and it increases serotonin in the brain. It creates effects of euphoria, emotional warmth, empathy, and heightened sensory perception. It appears to decrease defensiveness and numbing and helps people access their inner experience.[7] It can facilitate staying within a window of tolerance, so the person can revisit traumatic memories without being as overwhelmed physiologically or emotionally. This can be especially helpful in treating post-traumatic stress.

Researchers believe that psychedelics affect the brain by changing the neural connectivity and plasticity, impacting the role of serotonin receptors and the default mode network, which is associated with self-referential thought (how we perceive and engage with ourselves). Ketamine, a dissociative anesthetic, is already approved as an intervention for treatment-resistant depression.

More research is needed to fully assess the safety and potential risks of these kinds of therapies, but presently, research indicates that psychedelic-assisted therapies can produce significant improvements in symptoms for some individuals.[8,9] Responsibly guided treatments using these newer alternative medicines may become part of future treatment options.

ARTIFICIAL INTELLIGENCE (AI)

Current thoughts about using AI to get counseling advice include a mix of curiosity, serious concern, and caution. The potential benefits include readily available accessibility, low cost, and the anonymity that allows some people to feel more comfortable disclosing sensitive information to an AI chatbot without fear of being judged.

A number of companies are designing smartphone chatbots with input from trained therapists for use as an adjunct to treatment. The chatbots are specifically trained to respond with empathy and validation, to offer affirmations, to check in on the patient periodically, and to teach coping skills and strategies to feel better. These chatbots can analyze vast amounts of data and then potentially tailor interventions to the individual's needs. They can also track progress over time. Because these AI chatbots are being designed with the guidance of trained professionals who have patient safety top of mind, they show some promise.

Yet many question whether AI can really handle complex mental and emotional issues. One of the challenges and concerns includes the lack of genuine human empathy and connection, which is a crucial element of effective therapy, as well as an important part of other healing and fulfilling human relationships. The therapeutic alliance and human bond formed between a patient and their therapist is considered one of the most significant determinants of successful therapy.[10] While AI can simulate empathic language and provide information, it is not the same as the lived experience of being truly felt by another human being—a resonance that is foundational to emotional healing. Furthermore, AI-driven chatbots lack the critical discernment and intuition of a well-trained professional to pick up on the nuances, nonverbal cues, and complex subtexts that humans can better recognize.

There are obvious ethical considerations about data privacy and security as well, but probably the biggest concern is the potential for harm. The accuracy and reliability of AI-powered mental health tools are still being evaluated and there is a risk of misdiagnosis as well as harmful information or interventions. AI can make mistakes that could be costly, especially with people in vulnerable states. There have already been reports of suicide after people had been using AI as a therapist or confidant.[11]

At this point in time, we have more questions than answers. Will people become so reliant on the frictionless companionship or advice of AI that they struggle to navigate the messy, unpredictable, yet vital nature of real relationships that are so important to our well-being? Are we equipping people with the critical thinking skills they need to distinguish between algorithmic output and real wisdom and connection that enhances their lives? Will the business goals of AI trump the need for safety measures and regulations that should be considered and put in place? AI has the potential to play some useful roles in assisting individuals with their mental health concerns, but it's critical that we teach people to see it for what it is and proceed with caution to minimize the potential for harm.

Concluding Thoughts

Creating and maintaining improved mental health is a lifelong process. There is no one-size-fits-all solution or remedy. You'll need to experiment with various forms of available support and see what works best for you. Be persistent until you find the right combination of resources that help you develop yourself and improve your mental health. Keep in mind too that what you need may change over time depending on life circumstances. Don't be too shy or embarrassed to seek out help that supports your efforts to bring about meaningful transformation.

We're fortunate that there is now less stigma associated with seeking help and taking good care of your mental health. Many people—successful athletes, entrepreneurs, leaders in society—use therapists, coaches, and mentors of all kinds to help them not only deal with difficulties but also reach their potential and live life fully.

Too bad it has taken us so long as a society to realize the value of prioritizing mental health, given how dramatically it affects the way we all operate. Good mental health can develop naturally if you had enough good experiences to foster healthy development and did not have too many interfering factors. But remember, none of us are raised in flawless environments. Most of us have some deficits in our development and psychic pain or internal difficulties that need care and attention.

I hope that ongoing research will provide enough evidence to show insurance companies and the government that covering the expense of therapy and other preventative wellness programs and services would result in less money being spent on the treatment of other, more serious illnesses and problems. It pays off for everyone—individuals, families, and society—to invest in people's development and mental health because people with good mental health are better equipped to take care of their overall well-being, are more capable of coping with life's inevitable challenges, get along better with others, and are more likely to reach their full potential.

My hope is that you will feel inspired and empowered to make your mental health a priority. I hope you'll value and live as your authentic self, and use your mind, emotions, and relationships to enrich your life. May you navigate life's inevitable ups and downs with greater wisdom, joy, and resilience.

I wish you all the best on your journey. May you savor whatever goodness comes your way and be steady and strong when times are tough. I want to leave you with my own, more elaborate version of a shorter, well-known loving kindness meditation. I wrote it a few years after Wiley died during a time when I needed reminders of what was still possible—goodness within and around me—in spite of the sadness I still carried in my heart.

May I be filled with loving kindness
May I experience peace of mind and ease of the day
May I be of good health and good humor
May I be grateful and wise

May I be curious, compassionate, and mindfully present
May I be resilient in the face of life's challenges
May I have faith in the light and love within and around me
May I live with my mind and heart wide open

Appendix

A. Resources: Recommended Reading by Topic

B. Exercises

The Caring Behaviors Exercise

Identifying Your Strengths and Positive Qualities

Values Clarification Exercise

Questions to Understand Your Development

Self-Assessment: Your Essential Inner Resources

C. Additional Mental Health Resources

APPENDIX A

Resources: Recommended Reading by Topic

Emotional Capacities

Emotional Agility: Get Unstuck, Embrace Change, and Thrive in Life and Work (David, 2016)

Emotional Intelligence: Why It Can Matter More Than IQ (Goleman, 1995)

Permission to Feel: Unlocking the Power of Emotions to Help Our Kids, Ourselves, and Our Society Thrive (Brackett, 2019)

Resilience

Resilience: How to Grow an Unshakeable Core of Calm, Strength, and Happiness (Hanson, 2018)

Grit: The Power of Passion and Perseverance (Duckworth, 2016)

Mindset: The New Psychology of Success (Dweck, 2006)

Option B: Facing Adversity, Building Resilience, and Finding Joy (Sandberg and Grant, 2017)

A Lamp in the Darkness: Illuminating the Path Through Difficult Times (Kornfield, 2014)

Self-Compassion

Self-Compassion: The Proven Science of Being Kind to Yourself (Neff, 2011)

The Mindful Self-Compassion Workbook: A Proven Way to Accept Yourself, Build Inner Strength, and Thrive (Germer and Neff, 2018)

Good Morning, I Love You: Mindfulness and Self-Compassion Practices to Rewire Your Brain for Calm, Clarity and Joy (Shapiro, 2020)

Healthy Sense of Self

Making Room for the Disavowed (Wachtel, 2023)

No Bad Parts: Healing Trauma and Restoring Wholeness with the Family Systems Model (Schwartz, 2021)

Six Pillars of Self-Esteem (Brandon, 1994)

The Self-Esteem Workbook (Schiraldi, 2016)

The Gifts of Imperfection: Let Go of Who You Think You're Supposed to Be and Embrace Who You Are (Brown, 2010)

Mental Capacities

Attention Span: A Groundbreaking Way to Restore Balance, Happiness, and Productivity (Marks, 2023)

The Smart but Scattered Guide to Success: How to Use Your Brain's Executive Skills to Keep Up, Stay Calm, and Get Organized at Work and Home (Dawson & Guare, 2016)

Your Brain at Work: Strategies for Overcoming Distraction, Regaining Focus, and Working Smarter All Day Long (Rock, 2020)

Mindfulness and Meditation

Wherever You Go, There You Are: Mindfulness Meditation in Everyday Life (Kabat-Zinn, 1994)

Full Catastrophe Living: Using the Wisdom of Your Body and Mind to Face Stress, Pain, and Illness (Kabat-Zinn, 2013)

Relationships

Getting the Love You Want: A Guide for Couples (Hendrix and Hunt, 1988)

ACT with Love (Harris, 2021)

The Seven Principles for Making Marriage Work (Gottman and Silver, 1999)

Making Great Relationships (Hanson, 2023)

Grief and Loss

The Wild Edge of Sorrow: Rituals of Renewal and the Sacred Work of Grief (Weller, 2015)

The Grieving Brain (O'Connor, 2022)

Grief Works: Stories of Life, Death, and Surviving (Samuel, 2018)

Bearing the Unbearable: Love, Loss, and the Heartbreaking Path of Grief (Cacciatore, 2017)

I Wasn't Ready to Say Goodbye: Surviving, Coping, and Healing After the Sudden Death of a Loved One (Brook and Blair, 2000)

Trauma and Recovery

Journey Through Trauma: A Trail Guide to the 5-Phase Cycle of Healing Repeated Trauma (Schmelzer, 2018)

The Body Keeps the Score: Brain, Mind, and Body in the Healing of Trauma (van der Kolk, 2014)

Trauma and Recovery (Herman, 1992)

Flourishing and Fulfillment

The Power of Meaning: Finding Fulfillment in a World Obsessed with Happiness (Esfahani Smith, 2017)

Transcend: The New Science of Self-Actualization (Kaufman, 2020)

Man's Search for Meaning (Frankl, 1946)

Flourish: A Visionary New Understanding of Happiness and Well-Being (Seligman, 2011)

Happiness

The How of Happiness: A New Approach to Getting the Life You Want (Lyubomirsky, 2008)

Happier: Learn the Secrets to Daily Joy and Lasting Fulfillment (Ben-Shahar, 2007)

Build the Life You Want: The Art and Science of Getting Happy (Brooks and Winfrey, 2023)

The Happiness Hypothesis: Finding Modern Truth in Ancient Wisdom (Haidt, 2005)

APPENDIX B

The Caring Behaviors Exercise[1]

After each person in the relationship completes this exercise, share your lists with each other to help your partner understand what makes you feel loved and cared about. Your answers should describe concrete things that your partner can say or do to show love and care.

I feel loved and cared about when you ______________________

____

I feel loved and cared about when you______________________

____

I feel loved and cared about when you______________________

____

I feel loved and cared about when you ______________________

____

I feel loved and cared about when you ______________________

____

I feel loved and cared about when you ______________________

____

I feel loved and cared about when you______________________

____

I feel loved and cared about when you______________________

____

I feel loved and cared about when you ______________________

____

I feel loved and cared about when you ______________________

____

Listed below are examples using categories of common "languages of love."[2]

Words of Affirmation or Compliments: I feel loved and cared about when you say that you love me, or compliment me, and when you say thank you.

Acts of Service: I feel loved and cared about when you take care of paying the bills, help with chores without being asked, when you fix things for me, when you make meals for us, and take good care of our kids and home.

Quality Time: I feel loved and cared about when you plan dates for us, eat dinner with me each night and we talk about our day, when we take walks together, when we put our phones away when talking to each other, and when we take trips together.

Physical Touch: I feel loved and cared about when you give me a hug or when we kiss, make love, hold hands, rub each other's back, or snuggle on the couch or in bed when we read or watch a show together.

Gift-Giving: I feel loved and cared about when you buy me flowers for no reason or a gift when you're traveling, or you get me something you see just because you know how much I would like it, which makes me feel like you're thoughtfully holding me in mind and want to give me something tangible that sparks joy.

These suggestions can be things your partner has done in the past, is currently doing, or you wish they would learn to do. Rewrite or revise your lists once a year or when you notice your priorities and desires are changing.

Don't expect your partner to read your mind. Let them know what registers for you and how you prefer to have love demonstrated. You can also tell each other your preferred ways to give love. Try to find some middle ground between letting your partner show love in the ways they're most capable of and comfortable with and stretch yourself to give love in ways that the other person most enjoys. If you're finding it challenging to give and receive love in ways that work for both of you, I encourage you to seek the help of a couples therapist to figure out what may be making that so difficult.

Identifying Your Strengths and Positive Qualities

Healthy self-esteem includes being aware of and appreciating your strengths and positive qualities. We don't always show our best qualities daily, but circle at least ten traits you possess or are capable of. Ask others to point out your best qualities if you need help with this exercise. You can do this exercise with a degree of humility, knowing that, in addition to strengths, everyone has shortcomings and things about themselves that they can work to improve or change. We're all works in progress. Feel free to add items to the list.

Circle the traits and qualities that you possess or identify with:

Accomplished	Attractive	Conciliatory
Adventurous	Authentic	Conscientious
Affectionate	Calm	Consistent
Altruistic	Caring	Cooperative
Ambitious	Cheerful	Courageous
Analytic	Clever	Creative
Athletic	Compassionate	Curious

Deliberate
Determined
Diplomatic
Disciplined
Easy-going
Efficient
Emotionally mature
Empathic
Encouraging
Energetic
Enthusiastic
Ethical
Expressive
Fair
Flexible
Focused
Forgiving
Friendly
Funny
Generous
Gentle
Good attitude
Good communicator
Good friend
Good listener
Good partner
Grateful
Growth-oriented
Handy
Hard worker
Helpful
Honest
Humble
Imaginative
Insightful
Inspirational
Integrity
Intuitive
Kind
Leader
Likable
Logical
Love learning
Loving
Loyal
Mindful
Nurturing
Observant
Open-minded
Optimistic
Organized
Outgoing
Patient
Persuasive
Physically fit
Pioneering
Planner
Polite
Positive
Principled

Proactive

Problem solver

Punctual

Purpose-driven

Quirky

Rational

Reasonable

Reliable

Resilient

Respectful

Responsible

Self-aware

Self-confident

Sincere

Social

Spiritual

Spontaneous

Steady

Strategic

Strive for excellence

Strong

Supportive

Tactful

Talented

Team player

Thoughtful

Tidy

Trustworthy

Vibrant

Wise

Witty

Values Clarification Exercise

Living a Life Aligned with Your Values

Our values motivate us and influence our choices. The following writing exercise can help you identify and articulate your values.

A) Consider the following list of values and circle ten that are especially important to you. This list gives many examples, but it's not all inclusive. Feel free to write in your own:

- Connection, intimacy, romance, family, friendship, love
- Collaboration, participation, community, teamwork, communication
- Generosity, charity, contribution, responsiveness
- Freedom, personal power, independence, confidence, openness
- Strength, courage, resilience, determination, perseverance, emotional intelligence
- Authenticity, self-awareness, self-expression, assertiveness

- Learning, curiosity, growth, risk-taking, innovation, creativity, knowledge, wisdom
- Excellence, purpose, performance, success, recognition, control/self-regulation
- Productivity, organization, accuracy, order, focus, clarity, reliability, security
- Joy, adventure, fun, spontaneity, humor, zest, vitality, play, free spirit, aesthetics, beauty
- Integrity, honesty, tradition, trust, equanimity, justice, fairness, humility, prudence
- Spirituality, mindfulness, peace, simplicity, kindness, compassion, gratitude, harmony

B) List your top five values here:

C) Say something about why these values are important to you. If anyone played a significant role in shaping your values, what qualities do you admire about them and the way they live their life? Have certain life experiences helped you clarify what values resonate most deeply for you?

D) To live your life with greater intention aligned with your values, write down a few aspirations you have for each of these ten important areas of your life:

1. Health (physical, mental, emotional, spiritual)

2. Friendships and Social Life

3. Family Life and Relationships (immediate family, children, in-laws)

4. Primary Relationship

5. Personal Growth

6. Fun and Leisure, Hobbies

7. Career and Work

8. Finances

9. Home Environment

10. Sense of Purpose and Meaning

Explore the above questions with curiosity and self-compassion and on a scale of 1 to 10, rate how well you're doing at living in accordance with your hopes for each of these areas. Highlight areas that could use a little more attention.

What obstacles or challenges make it difficult to create or maintain what you desire for each area?

____

____

____

____

____

____

How well are your priorities, choices, and attitudes aligned with what you say you value?

____

____

____

____

____

____

List one thing you are willing to do differently that might bring you closer to fulfillment in each of the above ten areas of your life.

____

____

____

____

____

____

Questions to Understand Your Development

Identify Experiences That Shaped You and Your Ways of Being

For the sake of deeper self-awareness, consider writing responses to the following questions to understand what influenced the development of your sense of self and shaped your autopilot beliefs, patterns, expectations, coping strategies, and ways of operating that are now part of your conscious and unconscious mind. Some of the answers may not be immediately accessible but can become clearer over time as you make the effort to better understand yourself and your history.

1. How was your view of yourself and others influenced by the way that your caregivers, peers, relatives, and teachers/coaches treated you? Include both the affirming and belittling or negative messages you absorbed about yourself. What did their behavior teach you about others?

____

____

2. As a child, what aspects of yourself (feelings, desires, beliefs, behaviors, characteristics) were most welcomed? What parts of yourself did you feel you had to hide, disavow, or reject?

3. What attitudes and beliefs (positive and negative) did you learn growing up that organize the way you tend to see the world? For example, is your worldview fairly optimistic and hopeful or did your experiences leave you feeling more pessimistic or fearful?

4. What did you learn about giving and receiving love and care while growing up? Common ways of demonstrating love are acts of service, words of affirmation, gifts, quality time, and physical touch. How did your family members show love, positive regard, and affection?

5. What did you learn about forming connections with others? Were positive, reliable forms of attachment available? Did your interactions with your caregivers generally leave you feeling secure (confident, trusting), or did inconsistencies in their availability or a lack of warmth or safety leave you feeling more anxious (insecure, clinging), avoidant (detached), or disorganized

(fearful, confused)? Insight into your attachment style and new opportunities for healthier relating give you a chance to develop secure attachment style later in life (earned secure attachment).

____

____

____

____

____

____

6. How did you learn to handle conflict and anger (e.g., fight back, be passive, be aggressive, avoid conflict, be assertive, talk things through until some compromise or understanding was reached)? How did others in your family handle conflict?

____

____

____

____

____

____

7. How were disappointments and losses handled? What did you learn about grieving? Were losses in your life acknowledged and responded to with empathy? What were some difficult losses in your life, and have you processed and worked through them?

8. What are the coping strategies you resorted to in order to protect yourself from pain and disappointment or other unwanted feelings (e.g., denial, substance or alcohol use, food, rationalizations, retail therapy, working out, being in nature, prayer, writing, reaching out for help, etc.)? Identify the coping strategies you relied upon the most—the healthy ones and the ones that can cause problems in your life and need upgrading.

____

____

9. What values did your family encourage, model, or live by (e.g., excellence, hard work, obedience, learning, freedom, generosity, integrity, resilience, adventure, connection, collaboration, productivity, spirituality, etc.)?

____

____

____

____

____

____

This exercise can evoke uncomfortable feelings, especially if you're reminded of the ways your childhood was less than ideal. You may need time and help to compassionately mourn the losses and disappointments coming into your awareness.

Self-Assessment: Your Essential Inner Resources

Use this assessment to identify the capacities you'd like to work on for personal growth and to improve your mental health. These affirmations are reminders of what you are capable of or are working toward. Rate each statement using a scale of 1 to 3.

Scale:

1 = needs attention

2 = making progress or "good enough"

3 = this is a strength

A Healthy Sense of Self

SELF-AWARENESS

____ I have a good understanding of myself and how I came to be who I am.

____ I'm aware of how I tend to protect myself, try to get my needs met, deal with difficulties and conflict, and show love.

____ I reflect on my experience and try to make sense of it.

____ I can be honest with myself without being overly harsh or critical.

____ I use self-awareness to learn from my experience, redirect myself, heal, and grow.

SELF-ESTEEM

____ I accept, love, and value myself.

____ I have a healthy sense of pride for my efforts, accomplishments, competencies, and positive characteristics.

____ I have enough humility to admit when I'm wrong or misguided, and I'm aware of and willing to work on my shortcomings.

____ I use encouragement and supportive self-talk to motivate myself, instead of berating or belittling myself.

____ I compassionately face and work through the reasons I feel bad about myself, insecure, guilty, or ashamed.

____ I'm doing my best not to compare myself to others.

____ I accept who I am, an imperfect human, while doing what I can to develop myself into all of who I'm capable of becoming.

____ I talk to myself the same way I would to a friend I value, respect, and care about.

AUTHENTICITY

____ I'm free to be my most authentic self.

____ I'm careful not to sacrifice important parts of myself in order to be what others expect or want me to be, especially if it does not resonate with who I really am or want to be.

____ I accept all parts of myself, not just the most likeable parts.

____ I welcome back hidden or disavowed parts of myself so I can feel more whole and integrated.

____ I resist living as a "false self," showing only the best, most curated version of myself.

AGENCY

____ I act with intention to direct and influence my life in positive ways.

____ I know myself well enough to advocate for or pursue what matters to me.

____ I'm assertive.

____ I'm willing to face and deal with hard things.

____ I redirect myself as needed, using encouragement and discipline.

____ I have multiple ways of inviting pleasure into my everyday life so I'm not too dependent on any one source of pleasure that could become an addiction.

CORE VALUES AND A MORAL COMPASS

____ I have values and principles that act as a guide for my choices and decisions.

____ I try to align my actions with what truly matters, not just for the moment, but for the long run too.

____ I have a sense of right and wrong that allows me to cooperatively live in society with others.

____ I have empathy for others.

____ I learn from my mistakes and make amends when necessary.

COMPASSION

____ I meet my own suffering, and the suffering of others, with a kind, attentive presence and a spirit of compassionate responsiveness.

____ I can comfort and take good care of myself when I'm having a rough time.

MEANING AND PURPOSE

____ I find ways to live my life with a sense of purpose, orienting my life around personally meaningful values and goals.

____ I find meaning in my life and significance derived from connecting with and contributing to something larger than myself.

WISE, WARRIOR, AND LOVING SELF

____ I appreciate and rely on the parts of me capable of being wise, insightful, honest, loving, encouraging, empathic, kind, courageous, and resilient.

____ I allow the Wise Self to be the director of my life as often as possible and to mediate between all other parts of myself.

BALANCE OF ACCEPTANCE AND CHANGE

____ I'm finding some reasonable balance between accepting myself as I am and making efforts to work on aspects of myself that could use some attention and refinement.

Mental Capacities

SELF-REFLECTION AND INSIGHT

____ I'm capable of being aware of my state of mind. I can mindfully notice what is going on in my mind, without judgment.

____ I can generate insights and good guesses as to why I might be feeling, thinking, or acting as I am.

____ I can think things through and not be overly influenced by impulsive or automatic thoughts, stories, feelings, or urges.

____ I'm curious about my fluctuating states of mind and moods, and I try to be aware of the factors that influence my current mental and emotional state.

____ I'm able to be open-minded, reconsider my position, and broaden my perspective after taking in additional information.

OBSERVING YOUR MIND

____ I can observe what's going on in myself, and others, and not simply be hijacked by my racing mind or emotions.

____ I can simultaneously be having an experience and also observe it with curiosity.

____ I notice and can make educated guesses about other people's states of mind and why they may be behaving the way they are, which informs my options for how to interact with others.

____ I'm capable of pausing before reacting to intense feelings or thoughts.

FOCUS AND ATTENTION

____ I'm willing to practice skills that help me have greater control of my attention and racing mind, such as mindfulness, meditation, and breathing techniques.

____ I'm selective about the information I feed my mind and pay attention to the impact it has on my well-being.

GOOD JUDGMENT

____ I use good judgment and think about the consequences of my actions before deciding what to do.

STRATEGIZING, PLANNING, AND ORGANIZING

____ I use my mind to help me solve problems and adapt to unexpected changes.

____ I organize and manage my time to provide helpful direction and structure to my days.

____ I make plans and work toward goals. I can direct myself with intention.

____ I'm able to tolerate the hard parts of being disciplined in order to achieve my goals.

____ I'm developing and using the amazing capacities of my mind to help me live well, and I can change or modify thinking that is adding to my distress.

Emotional Capacities

RECOGNIZING AND ACKNOWLEDGING EMOTIONS

____ I appreciate the richness of my emotions and use them as one source of valuable information.

ACCEPTING AND TOLERATING YOUR EMOTIONAL EXPERIENCE

____ I can accept and tolerate my emotional experience however undesirable it may be.

____ I willingly allow myself to feel the full range of human emotion, spontaneous reactions to life events, without judgment.

____ I respond to emotions with curiosity and empathy and try to understand and appreciate why I feel the way I do.

REGULATING EMOTIONS

____ I have healthy ways of soothing myself when I am working through uncomfortable emotions.

____ I'm capable of challenging certain attitudes, thoughts, or stories I tell myself that exacerbate bad feelings and add unnecessary pain on top of real pain.

____ I pace myself when dealing with uncomfortable emotions and I take breaks from processing them as needed.

____ I courageously face and work through my feelings and the related issues they expose.

____ I respond to feelings with empathy and constructive action.

____ I use my emotions to understand myself and others better, and that understanding helps me temper reactivity.

____ I investigate the meaning of my emotions to make sense of things.

____ I use my emotions to motivate me to change what I can and learn valuable lessons.

Relational Capacities

AWARENESS AND INSIGHT

____ I know myself well enough to recognize my needs and preferences so I can advocate for them.

____ I'm aware of my particular sensitivities, tendencies, and protective strategies that can interfere with healthy relating, and I'm willing to work on them.

____ I'm learning to use healthier ways of getting my needs met and am willing to modify aversive methods I learned to use to influence others.

____ I'm using self-awareness and insight to help me mature into someone capable of building and maintaining good relationships (e.g., someone trustworthy, insightful, appreciative, respectful).

MUTUAL RECOGNITION

____ I recognize and respect that others have a separate and equally important mind of their own, with a distinct center of feeling and perception.

____ I aim to be empathic and strive to understand other people's experience and point of view, even when it's different from my own.

____ I work toward addressing differences in a way that leaves others feeling understood and taken into consideration.

____ I strive to work through differences and reach compromises both parties can live with, instead of trying to win arguments or insisting on getting my way.

____ I'm equally comfortable with my sense of separateness and autonomy as I am with closeness and intimacy.

EFFECTIVE COMMUNICATION

____ I communicate in ways that increase the likelihood of my message being heard and are less likely to evoke a defensive response.

____ I listen non-defensively and try to understand the other person's experience.

____ I'm honest and direct with others, and I say what I need to say as kindly as possible.

____ I can describe what upsets me, share how it makes me feel, and make a positive request for change that could improve the moment or situation.

____ I make an effort to repair things and make amends

when I contribute to misunderstandings, hurt feelings, or other interpersonal difficulties.

____ I focus my feedback on the behavior that hurts or concerns me, rather than attacking someone's character.

____ I suggest "time-outs" when a conversation is getting more negative or unproductive. I can ask that we reset and try again.

Healthy Coping Strategies

SELF-AWARENESS

____ I'm aware of the difference between healthy and unhealthy ways I try to protect myself from threatening or unpleasant experiences.

____ I make an effort to understand my automatic reactions and tendencies when I am upset or faced with a difficulty.

____ I notice when I'm starting to cope in unconstructive ways and make an effort to modify my approach.

ACCEPTANCE

____ I accept the realities of life.

____ I willingly and wisely accept the things I can't change or control.

____ I don't waste too much energy insisting that life be different than it is. I deal with what is.

COMPASSION AND SELF-CARE

____ I acknowledge the difficulty and pain I'm in, and I offer myself some compassion while I work through challenging experiences.

____ I take care of myself while I am in a distressed state so I can find the energy required to cope effectively with difficulties.

ATTITUDE

____ I believe in my capacity to work through hard things.

____ I praise myself for and encourage all efforts to constructively handle challenges.

____ I redirect overly negative thought loops or catastrophic thinking.

____ I challenge defeatist attitudes that interfere with a sense of hope, possibility, and determination.

CONSTRUCTIVE ACTION

____ I effectively cope with difficulties by taking constructive actions that help improve the moment or the situation.

____ I talk to myself with compassion and encouragement when facing something difficult, as I would talk to a good friend.

____ I avoid or redirect actions that might make things worse.

____ I stay solution-oriented when facing difficulties, using my energy for useful purposes such as self-soothing and problem-solving.

____ I turn to my inner Warrior Self to find the strength I need to face challenges.

____ I remember that I'm much more than my problems and that my resilience grows with each hard thing I face and work through.

APPENDIX C

Additional Mental Health Resources

CRISIS TEXT HOTLINE: 741741

You can text with trained crisis counselors any time of day or night.

SUICIDE AND CRISIS LIFELINE: CALL 988

Available 24/7 to speak by phone.

TREVOR PROJECT HOTLINE:

Free, confidential crisis intervention and suicide prevention services to LGBTQ+ youth (ages 13–24). Text 678-678 or call 1-866-488-7386

NAMI (NATIONAL ALLIANCE ON MENTAL ILLNESS):

1-800-950-NAMI (6264)

COMMUNAL ADDICTION RECOVERY OPTIONS:

Twelve-step programs, such as Alcoholics Anonymous (AA), provide support for a wide spectrum of addictive behaviors. Al-Anon is available to assist the addicted persons' loved ones.

Additionally, SMART Recovery and LifeRing offer a secular, non-spiritual approach to addressing addictive behavior. All three options are peer-led and accessible at no cost.

SAMHSA'S NATIONAL HELPLINE: SUBSTANCE ABUSE AND MENTAL HEALTH SERVICES ADMINISTRATION:

Confidential, free referral and information service for individuals and families facing mental and/or substance use disorders. Available 24/7 by phone.
1-800-662-HELP (4357)

AMERICAN FOUNDATION FOR SUICIDE PREVENTION (AFSP):

AFSP is a leading health organization dedicated to saving lives and bringing hope to those affected by suicide through research, advocacy, and support of survivors of suicide loss.
afsp.org

JED FOUNDATION:

Nonprofit organization working to promote good mental health in teens and young adults and prevent suicides.

jedfoundation.org

Acknowledgments

To the Reader

I am grateful to you for taking the time to engage with a book of this kind. I hope it has made a meaningful difference and helped you become better resourced to face life's challenges and live a fuller life.

My Patients

I want to thank all the patients I have had the privilege of working with. You have courageously made yourselves vulnerable, entrusting me with your deepest hopes, dreams, fears, and pain. I admire and respect your willingness to understand yourselves better, heal, invest in personal growth, and create a life that works for you. It has been an honor to be on the journey with you. (My patients' anonymity was preserved by changing their names and modifying enough details of their stories so they would not be identifiable.)

Mentors and Guides

I owe a huge debt of gratitude to my own therapists who have accompanied me on my journey of personal growth and healing. You have had such an important and meaningful impact on me. I appreciate all the mentors who have showed me how to be a good therapist.

Your investment and belief in me have made such a positive difference in my life, and I hope I am adequately paying it forward.

My Husband and Daughter

You have provided so much love, moral support, encouragement, and feedback on various drafts, as I worked on bringing this book to life. Words are not enough to express how much I love and appreciate both of you. Wendell, your belief in me and constant love are gifts I cherish. You are an amazing life partner. Elise, the combination of your big heart, emotional intelligence, and wisdom have enriched my life beyond measure. Your technical and practical support has been a welcome bonus too.

My Extended Family

I have been blessed with a loving family. We, like many families, have dealt with our fair share of difficulties and dysfunction, but an abiding love for one another runs deep. I am grateful to my father, an engineer, for teaching me to be a problem solver and put my mind to good use, and my mother was an amazing example of warmth, kindness, perseverance, and generosity. My siblings (Caroline, Larry, Denise, Matt, Susan, and Lisa), nieces and nephews, in-laws, and other relatives have enriched my life with their love and support. Thank you, family.

My "Book Support Team"

A special thanks to the early readers of my manuscript, who offered valuable feedback: Dr.'s Camilla Van Voorhees, Ric Almond, Jennifer Freed, and MaryAnn Zetes. Other generous souls cheered me on and helped with things one must do to get a book published—who knew it involved so much more than writing! Social media experts Kelsey Makaiwi and Julie Mrozinski, as well as Whitney Phaneuf and MeiMei Fox, who provided invaluable editing. A special thank you to Jessie and Amanda Birkhofer, Jackie Thompson, Amy Yates, Shawn Byers, Julie Brody, Jana Kahn, Peter Mazonson, Sally Lannin, Wendy Anderson, and Carrie Birkhofer—your extra support and enthusiasm for what I'm trying to accomplish with this book has been so meaningful.

To the team at Greenleaf Publishing Group—Justin Branch, Brian Welch, Maxine Marshall, Fallon Clark, Alyse Mervosh, Cameron Stein, Brittany Jones-Pugh, Madelyn Myers, Jamie White, Jen Jensen, and Gwen Cunningham: Your guidance and expertise has been invaluable. Thank you as well to the wonderful team at Fortier PR, Lauren Ortiz, Naja Innis, and Ian Antonoff.

I am profoundly grateful to the following colleagues who kindly provided generous endorsements for this book: Dr.'s Laura Roberts, Denise Pope, Stephanie Brown, Paul Wachtel, Tal Ben-Shahar, Shauna Shapiro, Laura Erickson-Schroth, Scott Kaufman, Steven C. Hayes, Harville Hendrix, Helen LaKelly Hunt, and Margaret Black Mitchell.

A Special Thank You to My Son Wiley

I take some comfort in imagining you, Wiley, as our special guardian. As a gifted writer yourself, I like to think that your inspiration was channeled through me as I wrote this book. My deepest hope is that the suffering you endured, and the lessons I've learned through my own journey, are being transformed into something truly helpful to others. I love you so much, Wiley, always, always.

Notes

Introduction: Take Care of Your Mental Health

1. Clark, A. E., Flèche, S., Layard, R., Powdthavee, N., & Ward, G. (2018). *The origins of happiness: The science of well-being over the life course.* Princeton University Press.
2. McGrath, J. J., Al-Hamzawi, A., Alonso, J., Altwaijri, Y., Andrade, L. H., Bromet, E. J., Bruffaerts, R., de Girolamo, G., de Jonge, P., Fayyad, J., Florescu, S., Gureje, O., Haro, J. M., Hu, C., Hu, L., Karam, E. G., Karam, G., Kessler, R. C., Kovess-Masfeti, V., . . . Viana, M. C. (2023). Age of onset and cumulative risk of mental disorders: A cross-national analysis of population surveys from 29 countries. *The Lancet Psychiatry*, 10(9), 668–681. https://doi.org/10.1016/S2215-0366(23)00193-1
3. Robins, L. N., & Regier, D. A. (1991). *Psychiatric disorders in America: The epidemiologic catchment area study.* The Free Press.
4. Substance Abuse and Mental Health Services Administration (SAMHSA). (2023). Key substance use and mental health indicators in the United States: Results from the 2022 National Survey on Drug Use and Health (HHS Publication No. PEP23–07–01–006, NSDUH Series H – 58). Center for Behavioral Health Statistics and Quality, Substance Abuse, and Mental Health Services Administration. https://www.samhsa.gov/data/sites/default/files/reports/rpt42731/2022-nsduh-nnr.pdf
5. Brenan, M. (2025, January 23). New low in U.S. "very satisfied" with personal life. *Gallup News*. https://news.gallup.com/poll/655493/new-low-satisfied-personal-life.aspx
6. Power, J. (2025, July 30). Share of people worldwide "thriving" hits new high, survey says. *Al Jazeera*. https://www.aljazeera.com/news/2025/7/30/share-of-people-worldwide-thriving-hits-new-high-survey-says

Chapter 1: Defining Good Mental Health, Fulfillment, Happiness, and the Essential Ingredients

1. Strümpfer, D. J. W. (1995). The salutogenic approach to health. *South African Journal of Psychology*, 25, 81–89.
2. U.S. Public Health Service. (1999). Mental health: A report of the Surgeon General. U.S. Department of Health and Human Services.
3. Lingiardi, V., & McWilliams, N. (Eds.). (2017). *Psychodynamic diagnostic manual: PDM-2*. Guilford Press.
4. Keyes, C. L. M. (2002). The mental health continuum: From languishing to flourishing in life. *Journal of Health and Social Behavior*, 43(2), 207–222. https://doi.org/10.2307/3090197
5. Keyes, C. L. M. (2005). Mental illness and/or mental health? Investigating axioms of the complete state model of health. *Journal of Consulting and Clinical Psychology*, 73(3), 539–548. https://doi.org/10.1037/0022-006X.73.3.539
6. Keyes, C. L. M. (2007). Promoting and protecting mental health as flourishing: A complementary strategy for improving national mental health. *American Psychologist*, 62(2), 95–108. https://pubmed.ncbi.nlm.nih.gov/17324035/
7. Ibid.
8. McGrath, J. J., Al-Hamzawi, A., Alonso, J., Altwaijri, Y., Andrade, L. H., Bromet, E. J., Bruffaerts, R., de Girolamo, G., de Jonge, P., Fayyad, J., Florescu, S., Gureje, O., Haro, J. M., Hu, C., Hu, L., Karam, E. G., Karam, G., Kessler, R. C., Kovess-Masfeti, V., . . . Viana, M. C. (2023). Age of onset and cumulative risk of mental disorders: A cross-national analysis of population surveys from 29 countries. *The Lancet Psychiatry*, 10(9), 668–681. https://doi.org/10.1016/S2215-0366(23)00193-1
9. U.S. Public Health Service. (1999). Mental health: A report of the Surgeon General. U.S. Department of Health and Human Services.
10. Snyderman, R., & Williams, R. S. (2003). Perspective medicine: The next healthcare transformation. *Academic Medicine*, 78, 1079–1084. https://pubmed.ncbi.nlm.nih.gov/14604864/
11. Steinberg Institute. (n.d.). Fact Sheet: The cost benefits of early intervention in mental illness. Retrieved from https://steinberginstitute.org/fact-sheet-cost-benefits-early-intervention-mental-illness/

12. U.S. Government Accountability Office. (2014, August 11). Health prevention: Cost-effective services in recent peer-reviewed health care literature (GAO-14-789R). https://www.gao.gov/products/gao-14-789r
13. Ryan, R., & Deci, E. (2000). Self-determination theory and the facilitation of intrinsic motivation, social development, and wellbeing. *American Psychologist*, 55, 68–78. https://psycnet.apa.org/doiLanding?doi =10.1037%2F0003-066X.55.1.68
14. Brown, S. (2014). *Speed: Facing our addiction to fast and faster—and overcoming our fear of slowing down*. Penguin Publishing Group.
15. Lembke, A. (2021). *Dopamine nation: Finding balance in the age of indulgence*. Dutton, an imprint of Penguin Random House LLC.
16. Ryff, C. D. (1995). Psychological well-being in adult life. *Current directions in psychological science*, 4, 99–104. https://doi.org/10.1111/1467-8721 .ep10772395
17. Seligman, M. E. P. (2011). *Flourish: A visionary new understanding of happiness and well-being*. Free Press.
18. Baumann, D., & Ruch, W. (2022). What constitutes a fulfilled life? A mixed methods study on lay perspectives across the lifespan. *Frontiers in Psychology*, 13, 982782. https://doi.org/10.3389/fpsyg.2022.982782
19. Huta, V., & Ryan, R. M. (2010). Pursuing pleasure or virtue: The differential and overlapping well-being benefits of hedonic and eudaimonic motives. *Journal of Happiness Studies*, 11(6), 735–762.
20. Shedler, J., & Westen, D. (2007). The Shedler-Westen Assessment Procedure (SWAP): Making personality diagnosis clinically meaningful. *Journal of Personality Assessment*, 89, 41–55. https://doi.org/10.1080/00223890701357092

Chapter 2: An Introduction to the Mind and Development

1. Siegel, D. J. (1999). *The developing mind: Toward a neurobiology of interpersonal experience*. Guilford Press.
2. Cowen, A. S., & Keltner, D. (2017). Self-report captures 27 distinct categories of emotion bridged by continuous gradients. *Proceedings of the National Academy of Sciences*, 114(38), E7900–E7909. https://doi.org/10.1073/pnas.1702247114

3. Bargh, J. A., & Chartrand, T. L. (1999). The unbearable automaticity of being. *American Psychologist*, 54(7), 462–479. https://psycnet.apa.org/doi/10.1037/0003-066X.54.7.462
4. Solms, M. (2018). The scientific standing of psychoanalysis. *Frontiers in Behavioral Neuroscience,* 12, 294. https://doi.org/10.1192/bji.2017.4
5. Maslow, A. H. (1943). A theory of human motivation. *Psychological Review*, 50(4), 370–396. https://doi.org/10.1037/h0054346
6. Lichtenberg, J. D. (1989). *Psychoanalysis and motivation.* Analytic Press.
7. Panksepp, J. (1998). *Affective neuroscience: The foundations of human and animal emotions.* Oxford University Press.
8. Kaufman, S. B. (2020). *Transcend: The new science of self-actualization.* Penguin Publishing Group.
9. Felitti, V. J., Anda, R. F., Nordenberg, D., Williamson, D. F., Spitz, A. M., Edwards, V., Koss, M. P., & Marks, J. S. (1998). Relationship of childhood abuse and household dysfunction to many of the leading causes of death in adults: The Adverse Childhood Experiences (ACE) Study. *American Journal of Preventive Medicine*, 14(4), 245–258. https://www.ajpmonline.org/article/S0749-3797(98)00017-8/fulltext#:~:text=10.1016/S0749%2D3797(98)00017%2D8
10. Ibid.

Chapter 3: Your Sense of Self and Its Parts

1. Dweck, C. S. (2006). *Mindset: The new psychology of success.* Random House.
2. Dane, A., & Bhatia, K. (2023). The social media diet: A scoping review to investigate the association between social media, body image and eating disorders amongst young people. *PLOS Global Public Health*, 3(3), e0001091. https://doi.org/10.1371/journal.pgph.0001091
3. Suler, J. (2004). The online disinhibition effect. *Cyberpsychology & Behavior*, 7(3), 321–326.
4. Schwartz, R. (2021). *No bad parts: Healing trauma and restoring wholeness with the internal family systems model.* Sounds True.
5. Bromberg, P. M. (1999). *Standing in the spaces: Essays on clinical process trauma and dissociation.* Routledge.

6. Wachtel, P. L. (2023). *Making room for the disavowed: Reclaiming the self in psychotherapy.* Guilford Press.

Chapter 4: A Healthy Sense of Self

1. Linehan, M. M. (2015). *DBT skills training manual* (2nd ed.). Guilford Press.
2. Ryff, C. D. (1995). Psychological well-being in adult life. *Current Directions in Psychological Science*, 4, 99–104.
3. Neff, K. D. (2011). *Self-compassion: The proven power of being kind to yourself.* William Morrow.
4. Hayes, S. C. (2019). *A liberated mind: How to pivot toward what matters.* Ebury Publishing.
5. Neff, K. D., & Germer, C. K. (2018). *The mindful self-compassion workbook: A guide to developing inner strength for lasting happiness.* Guilford Press.
6. Dweck, C. S. (2006). *Mindset.* Random House.
7. Linehan, M. M. (2015). *DBT skills training manual* (2nd ed.). Guilford Press.

Chapter 5: Mental Capacities

1. Burke Harris, N. (2018). *The deepest well: Healing the long-term effects of childhood adversity.* Houghton Mifflin Harcourt.
2. Kabat-Zinn, J. (2013). *Full catastrophe living: Using the wisdom of your body and mind to face stress, pain, and illness.* Bantam Dell.
3. Basso, J. C., McHale, A., Ende, V., Oberlin, D. J., & Suzuki, W. A. (2019). Brief daily meditation enhances attention, memory, mood, and emotion regulation in non-experienced meditators. *Behavioral Brain Research*, 356, 208–220. https://doi.org/10.1016/j.bbr.2018.08.023

Chapter 6: Emotional Capacities

1. Taylor, J. B. (2008). *My stroke of insight: A brain scientist's personal journey.* Viking.
2. Kabat-Zinn, J. (2013). *Full catastrophe living: Using the wisdom of your body and mind to face stress, pain, and illness.* Bantam Dell.

3. Kross, Ethan. (2025). *Shift: Managing your emotions—so they don't manage you.* Crown.
4. Gore, F. M., et al. (2023). Brief structured respiration practices enhance mood and reduce physiological arousal. *Cell Reports Medicine*, 4(1), 100895. doi: 10.1016/j.xcrm.2022.100895
5. Fincham, G., et al. (2023). Effect of breathwork on stress and mental health: A meta-analysis of randomized-controlled trials. *Scientific Reports*, 13, Article number: 7300. doi:10.1038/s41598-022-27247-y
6. van der Kolk, B. A. (2014). *The body keeps the score: Brain, mind, and body in the healing of trauma.* Viking.
7. Ibid.
8. Stolorow, R. D., & Atwood, G. E. (1992). Contexts of being: The intersubjective foundations of psychological life. The Analytic Press.

Chapter 7: Relational Capacities

1. Waldinger, R., & Schulz, M. (2023). *The good life: Lessons from the world's longest scientific study of happiness.* Simon & Schuster.
2. Lyons-Ruth, K. (1999). The two-person unconscious: Intersubjective dialogue, enactive relational representation, and the emergence of new forms of relational organization. *Psychoanalytic Inquiry*, 19, 576–617. https://doi.org/10.1080/07351699909534267
3. Goleman, D. (1995). *Emotional intelligence: Why it can matter more than IQ.* Bantam Books.
4. Gottman, J. M. (1999). *The seven principles for making marriage work: A practical guide from the country's foremost relationship expert.* Harmony Books.
5. Brown, B. (2012). *Daring greatly: How the courage to be vulnerable transforms the way we live, love, parent, and lead.* Gotham Books.
6. Benjamin, J. (1988). *The bonds of love: Psychoanalysis, feminism, and the problem of domination.* Pantheon Books.
7. Caspi, A., Roberts, B.W., & Shiner, R. L. (2005). Personality development: Stability and change. *Annual Review of Psychology*, 56, 453–484. DOI: 10.1146/annurev.psych.55.090902.141913

8. Benjamin, J. (1988). *The bonds of love: Psychoanalysis, feminism, and the problem of domination.* Pantheon Books.
9. Laitinen, A. (2022). Mutual recognition and well-being: What is it for relational selves to thrive? In *The theory and practice of recognition.* Routledge.
10. Gottman, J.M., & DeClaire, J. (2001). *The relationship cure: A 5 step guide to strengthening your marriage, family, and friendship.* Harmony Books.
11. Rosenberg, M. B. (2015). *Nonviolent communication: A language of life* (3rd ed.). PuddleDancer Press.
12. Gottman, J. M. (1999). *The seven principles for making marriage work: A practical guide from the country's foremost relationship expert.* Harmony Books.
13. Ibid
14. Hendrix, H., & Hunt, H. L. (2019). *Getting the love you want: A guide for couples* (3rd edition). St. Martin's Griffin.
15. Chapman, G. D. (2010). *The 5 love languages: The secret to love that lasts.* Northfield Publishing.

Chapter 8: Healthy Coping Strategies

1. Dweck, C. S. (2006). *Mindset.* Random House.
2. Calhoun, L. G., & Tedeschi, R. G. (2012). *Posttraumatic growth in clinical practice.* Routledge.
3. Werner, E. E. (1982). *Vulnerable but invincible: A longitudinal study of resilient children and youth.* McGraw-Hill.
4. Ryan, R., & Deci, E. (2000). Self-determination theory and the facilitation of intrinsic motivation, social development, and wellbeing. *American Psychologist,* 55, 68–78. DOI: 10.1037//0003-066x.55.1.68
5. Maslow, A. (1970). *Motivation and personality.* Harper & Row.
6. Felitti, V. J., Anda, R. F., Nordenberg, D., Williamson, D. F., Spitz, A. M., Edwards, V., Koss, M. P., & Marks, J. S. (1998). Relationship of childhood abuse and household dysfunction to many of the leading causes of death in adults: The Adverse Childhood Experiences (ACE) Study. *American Journal of Preventive Medicine,* 14(4), 245–258. DOI: 10.1016/s0749-3797(98)00017-8

7. Frankl, V. E., (2006). *Man's search for meaning*. Beacon Press. (Original work published in 1946).
8. Lamott, A. (2005). *Plan B: Further thoughts on faith*. Riverhead Books.

Chapter 9: Your Journey of Personal Growth and Development

1. Duncan, B. L., Miller, S. D., Wampold, B. E., & Hubble, M. A. (Eds.). (2010). *The heart and soul of change: Delivering what works in therapy* (2nd ed.). American Psychological Association.
2. Hayes, S. C., Strosahl, K. D., & Wilson, K. G., (2012) *Acceptance and commitment therapy: The process and practice of mindful change* (2nd ed.). Guilford Press.
3. Schwartz, R. (2021). *No bad parts: Healing trauma and restoring wholeness with the internal family systems model.* Sounds True.
4. Linehan, M. M. (2015). *DBT skills training manual* (2nd ed.). Guilford Press.
5. Koenig, H. G. (2012). *Spirituality and health research: Methods, measurements, health outcomes, and applications.* Templeton Press.
6. Multidisciplinary Association for Psychedelic Studies. (2021, February). *A multi-site phase 3 study of MDMA-assisted psychotherapy for PTSD.* ClinicalTrials.gov. https://clinicaltrials.gov/ct2/show/NCT04077437
7. Mithoefer, M. C., Feduccia, A. A., Jerome, L., Mithoefer, A., Wagner, M., Walsh, Z., Hamilton, S., Yazar-Klosinski, B., Emerson, A., & Doblin, R. (2019). MDMA-assisted psychotherapy for treatment of PTSD: Study design and rationale for phase 3 trials based on pooled analysis of six phase 2 randomized controlled trials. *Psychopharmacology*, 236(9), 2735–2745. DOI: 10.1007/s00213-019-05249-5
8. Griffiths, R. R., Johnson, M. W., Carducci, M. A., Umbricht, A., Richards, W. A., Richards, B. D., Cosimano, M. P., & Klinedinst, M. A. (2016). Psilocybin produces substantial and sustained decreases in depression and anxiety in patients with life-threatening cancer: A randomized, double-blind, placebo-controlled trial. *Journal of Psychopharmacology*, 30(12), 1181–1197. DOI: 10.1177/0269881116675513
9. Mithoefer et al. (2019).

10. Duncan, B. L., Miller, S. D., Wampold, B. E., & Hubble, M. A. (2009). *The heart and soul of change: Delivering what works in therapy* (2nd ed.). American Psychological Association.

11. CBS News. (2025, September 16). Parents of teens who died by suicide after AI chatbot interactions testify in Congress. https://www.cbsnews.com/news/ai-chatbots-teens-suicide-parents-testify-congress/

Appendix: The Caring Behavior Exercise

12. Hendrix, H., & Hunt, H. L. (2019). *Getting the love you want: A guide for couples* (3rd edition). St. Martin's Griffin.

13. Chapman, G. D. (2010). *The 5 love languages: The secret to love that lasts.* Northfield Publishing.

Bibliography

Bargh, J. A., & Chartrand, T. L. (1999). The unbearable automaticity of being. *American Psychologist,* 54(7), 462–479.

Basso, J. C., McHale, A., Ende, V., Oberlin, D. J., & Suzuki, W. A. (2019). Brief daily meditation enhances attention, memory, mood, and emotion regulation in non-experienced meditators. *Behavioral Brain Research,* 356, 208–220. https://doi.org/10.1016/j.bbr.2018.08.023

Baumann, D., & Ruch, W. (2022). What constitutes a fulfilled life? A mixed methods study on lay perspectives across the lifespan. *Frontiers in Psychology,* 13, 982782.

Benjamin, J. (1988). *The bonds of love: Psychoanalysis, feminism, and the problem of domination.* Pantheon Books.

Brenan, M. (2025, January 22). *New low in U.S. "very satisfied" with personal life. Gallup News.* https://news.gallup.com/poll/655493/new-low-satisfied-personal-life.aspx

Bromberg, P. M. (1999). *Standing in the spaces: Essays on clinical process trauma and dissociation.* Routledge.

Brown, B. (2012). *Daring greatly: How the courage to be vulnerable transforms the way we live, love, parent, and lead.* Gotham Books.

Brown, S. (2014). *Speed: Facing our addiction to fast and faster—and overcoming our fear of slowing down.* Penguin Publishing Group.

Burke Harris, N. (2018). *The deepest well: Healing the long-term effects of childhood adversity.* Houghton Mifflin Harcourt.

Calhoun, L. G., & Tedeschi, R. G. (2012). *Posttraumatic growth in clinical practice.* Routledge.

Caspi, A., Roberts, B.W., & Shiner, R. L. (2005). Personality development: Stability and change. *Annual Review of Psychology*, 56, 453–484.

CBS News. (2025, September 16). Parents of teens who died by suicide after AI chatbot interactions testify in Congress. https://www.cbsnews.com/news/ai-chatbots-teens-suicide-parents-testify-congress/

Chapman, G. D. (2010). *The 5 love languages: The secret to love that lasts.* Northfield Publishing.

Clark, A. E., Flèche, S., Layard, R., Powdthavee, N., & Ward, G. (2018). *The origins of happiness: The science of well-being over the life course.* Princeton University Press.

Cowen, A. S., & Keltner, D. (2017). Self-report captures 27 distinct categories of emotion bridged by continuous gradients. *Proceedings of the National Academy of Sciences*, 114(38), E7900–E7909.

Dane, A., & Bhatia, K. (2023). The social media diet: A scoping review to investigate the association between social media, body image, and eating disorders amongst young people. *PLOS Global Public Health*, 3(3), e0001091. https://doi.org/10.1371/journal.pgph.0001091

Duncan, B. L., Miller, S. D., Wampold, B. E., & Hubble, M. A. (2009). *The heart and soul of change: Delivering what works in therapy* (2nd ed.). American Psychological Association.

Dweck, C. S. (2006). *Mindset*. Random House.

Felitti, V. J., Anda, R. F., Nordenberg, D., Williamson, D. F., Spitz, A. M., Edwards, V., Koss, M. P., & Marks, J. S. (1998). Relationship of childhood abuse and household dysfunction to many of the leading causes of death in adults: The Adverse Childhood Experiences (ACE) Study. *American Journal of Preventive Medicine*, 14(4), 245–258.

Fincham, G., et al. (2023). Effect of breathwork on stress and mental health: A meta-analysis of randomized-controlled trials. *Scientific Reports*, 13, Article number: 7300.

Frankl, V. E, (2006). *Man's search for meaning*. Beacon Press. (Original work published in 1946).

Goleman, D. (1995). *Emotional intelligence: Why it can matter more than IQ*. Bantam Books.

Gore, F. M., et al. (2023). Brief structured respiration practices enhance mood and reduce physiological arousal. *Cell Reports Medicine*, 4(1), 100892.

Gottman, J. M. (1999). *The seven principles for making marriage work: A practical guide from the country's foremost relationship expert*. Harmony Books.

Gottman, J. M., & DeClaire, J. (2001). *The relationship cure: A 5 step guide to strengthening your marriage, family and friendship*. Harmony Books.

Griffiths, R. R., Johnson, M. W., Carducci, M. A., Umbricht, A., Richards, W. A., Richards, B. D., Cosimano, M. P., & Klinedinst, M. A. (2016). Psilocybin produces substantial and sustained decreases in depression and anxiety in patients with life-threatening cancer: A randomized, double-blind, placebo-controlled trial. *Journal of Psychopharmacology*, 30(12), 1181–1197.

Hayes, S. C. (2019). *A liberated mind: How to pivot toward what matters*. Ebury Publishing.

Hayes, S. C., Strosahl, K. D., & Wilson, K. G., (2012) *Acceptance and commitment therapy: The process and practice of mindful change* (2nd ed.). Guilford Press.

Hendrix, H., & Hunt, H. L. (2019). *Getting the love you want: A guide for couples* (3rd edition). St. Martin's Griffin.

Huta, V., & Ryan, R. M. (2010). Pursuing pleasure or virtue: The differential and overlapping well-being benefits of hedonic and eudaimonic motives. *Journal of Happiness Studies*, 11(6), 735–762.

Kabat-Zinn, J. (2013). *Full catastrophe living: Using the wisdom of your body and mind to face stress, pain, and illness.* Bantam Dell.

Kaufman, S. B. (2020). *Transcend: The new science of self-actualization.* Penguin Publishing Group.

Keyes, C. L. M. (2002). The mental health continuum: From languishing to flourishing in life. *Journal of Health and Social Behavior*, 43(2), 207–222.

Keyes, C. L. M. (2005). Mental illness and/or mental health? Investigating axioms of the complete state model of health. *Journal of Consulting and Clinical Psychology*, 73(3), 539–548.

Keyes, C. L. M. (2007). Promoting and protecting mental health as flourishing: A complementary strategy for improving national mental health. *American Psychologist*, 62(2), 95–108. https://pubmed.ncbi.nlm.nih.gov/17324035/

Keyes, C. L. M., & Grzywacz, J. G. (2005). Health as a complete state: The added value in work performance and healthcare costs. *Journal of Occupational and Environmental Medicine*, 47(5), 523–532.

Koenig, H. G. (2012). *Spirituality and health research: Methods, measurements, health outcomes, and applications.* Templeton Press.

Kross, E. (2025). *Shift: Managing your emotions—so they don't manage you.* Crown.

Laitinen, A. (2022). Mutual recognition and well-being: What is it for relational selves to thrive? In *The theory and practice of recognition.* Routledge.

Lamott, A. (2005). *Plan B: Further thoughts on faith.* Riverhead Books.

Lembke, A. (2021). *Dopamine nation: Finding balance in the age of indulgence.* Dutton, an imprint of Penguin Random House LLC.

Lichtenberg, J. D. (1989). *Psychoanalysis and motivation.* Analytic Press.

Linehan, M. M. (2015). *DBT skills training manual* (2nd ed.). Guilford Press.

Lingiardi, V., & McWilliams, N. (Eds.). (2017). *Psychodynamic diagnostic manual: PDM-2*. Guilford Press.

Lyons-Ruth, K. (1999). The two-person unconscious: Intersubjective dialogue, enactive relational representation, and the emergence of new forms of relational organization. *Psychoanalytic Inquiry*, 19, 576–617.

Lyubomirsky, S. (2007). *The how of happiness: A scientific approach to getting the life you want*. Penguin Press.

Maslow, A. H. (1943). A theory of human motivation. *Psychological Review*, 50(4), 370–396.

Maslow, A. (1970). *Motivation and personality*. Harper & Row.

McGrath, J. J., Al-Hamzawi, A., Alonso, J., Altwaijri, Y., Andrade, L. H., Bromet, E. J., Bruffaerts, R., de Girolamo, G., de Jonge, P., Fayyad, J., Florescu, S., Gureje, O., Haro, J. M., Hu, C., Hu, L., Karam, E. G., Karam, G., Kessler, R. C., Kovess-Masfeti, V., . . . & Viana, M. C. (2023). Age of onset and cumulative risk of mental disorders: A cross-national analysis of population surveys from 29 countries. *The Lancet Psychiatry*, 10(9), 668–681. https://doi.org/10.1016/S2215-0366(23)00193-1

Mithoefer, M. C., Feduccia, A. A., Jerome, L., Mithoefer, A., Wagner, M., Walsh, Z., Hamilton, S., Yazar-Klosinski, B., Emerson, A., & Doblin, R. (2019). MDMA-assisted psychotherapy for treatment of PTSD: Study design and rationale for phase 3 trials based on pooled analysis of six phase 2 randomized controlled trials. *Psychopharmacology*, 236(9), 2735–2745.

Multidisciplinary Association for Psychedelic Studies. (2021, February). *A multi-site phase 3 study of MDMA-assisted psychotherapy for PTSD*. ClinicalTrials.gov. https://clinicaltrials.gov/ct2/show/NCT04077437

Neff, K. D. (2011). *Self-compassion: The proven power of being kind to yourself*. William Morrow.

Neff, K. D., & Germer, C. K. (2018). *The mindful self-compassion workbook: A guide to developing inner strength for lasting happiness.* Guilford Press.

Panksepp, J. (1998). *Affective neuroscience: The foundations of human and animal emotions.* Oxford University Press.

Power, J. (2025, July 30). Share of people worldwide "thriving" hits new high, survey says. *Al Jazeera.* https://www.aljazeera.com/news/2025/7/30/share-of-people-worldwide-thriving-hits-new-high-survey-says

Robins, L. N., & Regier, D. A. (1991). *Psychiatric disorders in America: The epidemiologic catchment area study.* The Free Press.

Rosenberg, M. B. (2015). *Nonviolent communication: A language of life* (3rd ed.). PuddleDancer Press.

Ryan, R., & Deci, E. (2000). Self-determination theory and the facilitation of intrinsic motivation, social development, and wellbeing. *American Psychologist,* 55, 68–78.

Ryan, R. M., & Deci, E. L. (2001). On happiness and human potentials: A review of research on hedonic and eudaimonic well-being. *Annual Review of Psychology,* 52, 141–166.

Ryff, C. D. (1995). Psychological well-being in adult life. *Current Directions in Psychological Science,* 4, 99–104.

Schwartz, R. (2021). *No bad parts: Healing trauma and restoring wholeness with the internal family systems model.* Sounds True.

Seligman, M. E. P. (2011). *Flourish: A visionary new understanding of happiness and well-being.* Free Press.

Shedler, J., & Westen, D., (2007). The Shedler-Westen Assessment Procedure (SWAP): Making personality diagnosis clinically meaningful. *Journal of Personality Assessment,* 89, 41–55.

Sheldon, K. M., & Kasser, T. (1998). Pursuing personal goals: Skills enable progress, but not all progress is beneficial. *Journal of Personality and Social Psychology,* 75(6), 1319–1331.

Siegel, D. J. (1999). *The developing mind: Toward a neurobiology of interpersonal experience*. Guilford Press.

Snyderman, R., & Williams, R. S. (2003). Perspective medicine: The next healthcare transformation. *Academic Medicine*, 78, 1079–1084.

Solms, M. (2018). The scientific standing of psychoanalysis. *Frontiers in Behavioral Neuroscience*, 12, 294.

Steinberg Institute. (n.d.). *Fact sheet: The cost benefits of early intervention in mental illness*. Retrieved from https://steinberginstitute.org/fact-sheet-cost-benefits-early-intervention-mental-illness/

Stolorow, R. D., & Atwood, G. E. (1992). *Contexts of being: The intersubjective foundations of psychological life*. The Analytic Press.

Strümpfer, D. J. W. (1995). The salutogenic approach to health. *South African Journal of Psychology*, 25, 81–89.

Substance Abuse and Mental Health Services Administration (SAMHSA). (2023). Key substance use and mental health indicators in the United States: Results from the 2022 National Survey on Drug Use and Health (HHS Publication No. PEP23–07–01–006, NSDUH Series H–58.) Center for Behavioral Health Statistics and Quality, Substance Abuse, and Mental Health Services Administration. https://www.samhsa.gov/data/report/2022-annual-national-report

Suler, J. (2004). The online disinhibition effect. *Cyberpsychology & Behavior*, 7(3), 321–326.

Taylor, J. B. (2008). *My stroke of insight: A brain scientist's personal journey*. Viking.

U.S. Government Accountability Office. (2014, August 11). Health prevention: Cost-effective services in recent peer-reviewed health care literature (GAO-14-789R). https://www.gao.gov/products/gao-14-789r

U.S. Public Health Service. (1999). Mental health: A report of the Surgeon General. U.S. Department of Health and Human Services.

van der Kolk, B. A. (2014). *The body keeps the score: Brain, mind, and body in the healing of trauma*. Viking.

Wachtel, P. L. (2023). *Making room for the disavowed: Reclaiming the self in psychotherapy*. Routledge.

Waldinger, R., & Schulz, M. (2023). *The good life: Lessons from the world's longest scientific study of happiness*. Simon & Schuster.

Werner, E. E. (1982). *Vulnerable but invincible: A longitudinal study of resilient children and youth*. McGraw-Hill.

Index

A

AA (Alcoholics Anonymous), 208
acceptance
  balancing change and, 52–54, 64
  of emotional experience, 84–85, 97
  exercise, 142–143
  healthy coping, 133–134, 138
  self-assessment, 197, 204–205
Acceptance and Commitment Therapy (ACT), 155
accomplishments, 16
active listening, 110
acts of service, 172
addictions, 15
adrenaline, 90
adverse childhood experiences, 25, 26, 27–29
advocating for self, 104–105
affective processes, 11
affirmation, 172
AFSP (American Foundation for Suicide Prevention), 208
agency in healthy sense of self
  overview, 50–51
  self-assessment, 62–63, 195–196
Alcoholics Anonymous (AA), 208
alternative mental health resources, 156–162
American Foundation for Suicide Prevention (AFSP), 208
Anne of Green Gables (Montgomery), 33
anxiety
  coping with, 90–93
  despising and fearing, 91
  development of disorders, 92
  fight, fawn, or freeze response, 90
  illusion of safety, 92
  questions to understand, 91–92
  worrying as control, 92
apathetic withdrawal, 126
apologies, 110
apps, mental health, 157–159
artificial intelligence (AI), 160–162
assertiveness, 104
attachment style, 44
attention
  challenge of, 72–73
  exercise, 78
  mindfulness and meditation, 73
  self-assessment, 199
attitudes
  exercise, 143
  healthy coping, 135–136, 138
  self-assessment, 205
  and sense of self, 43–44
authentic sense of self, 40–43
authenticity
  and happiness, 16
  in healthy sense of self, 49–50
  self-assessment, 62, 195
autopilot, 20–22, 26–27, 31, 48

avoidance, 53–54, 125–126
awareness. *See also* self-awareness
  advocating for self, 104–105
  emotional maturity, 102
  exercise, 120
  insight, 102
  of others' states of mind, 102–103
  and personal growth, 101–105
  self-assessment, 202
  of strategies to influence people, 103–104

B

behavioral therapies, 153
beliefs and sense of self, 43–44
biological deficits, 124, 146
biological needs, 23
biological-based interventions, 156
Birkhofer, Celeste, 1–2, 164
Birkhofer, Wiley, 2–3, 139–140, 164, 211
black-and-white thinking, 128–129
blaming, 129
books as mental health resource, 157
brain-stimulation treatments, 156
breaks, taking, 87–88

C

Camus, Albert, 123
caregivers
  influence on sense of self, 34–37, 43
  role in development, 23–24
caring behaviors exercise, 171–173
catastrophizing, 87, 135
change. *See also* personal growth
  balancing self-acceptance and, 52–54, 64
  difficulty of, 146–147
  self-assessment, 197
chatbots, 160–161
childhood trauma
  effects of, 25–26, 27–29
  and sense of self, 54
cognitive behavioral therapy (CBT), 153, 154
cognitive processes, 11
communication
  effective, 107–114
  exercise, 121–122
  foundational importance of, 107
  general tips for, 113–114
  listening to understand, 110–111
  monitoring process, 111–113
  provoking defensiveness, 107–108
  repairing ruptures, 112–113
  self-assessment, 203–204
  three basic steps for, 108–110, 113
comparisons, 35–36
compassion
  in healthy sense of self, 51–52, 63
  self-assessment, 196, 205
  self-care, 134–135, 138, 143
  self-soothing, 86
competitiveness, 37
compliments, 172
conflict and sense of self, 44
consciousness, 20
constructive action
  in healthy coping strategies, 136–138
  self-assessment, 144, 206
control
  influence on relationships, 103
  tactics, 126–128
  and worrying, 92
coping. *See also* healthy coping strategies
  and autopilot, 20–21

in good mental health, 11
and sense of self, 44–45
core values in healthy sense of self, 51, 63
cortisol, 90
courage
and advocating for self, 104
and attitude, 135
and change, 54
meeting emotions with, 88
and new experiences, 149
crises, 157–158
Crisis Text Line, 158, 207
critical thinking, 162
criticism, 35–36, 103
cruelty, ease of online, 39
curiosity
acknowledging emotions, 84
and insight, 148
meeting emotions with, 89
observing mind, 70
and self-state, 41
and self-talk, 55

D

declarative knowledge, 100
defense mechanisms, 90, 130
defenses in good mental health, 11
demanding, 103
denial, 128–129
devaluation, 129
development. *See also* personal growth
and change, 26–27
introduction to, 22–31
Mia's story, 26
as ongoing process, 31–32
questions to understand, 187–192
of sense of self, 34–37, 38–40, 43–45
Sophia's story, 26–31
Dialectic Behavior Therapy (DBT), 155
disavowal, 128–129
discounting, 103
dissociation, 128
dopamine, 15

E

efficiency of mind, 20–22
electroconvulsive therapy (ECT), 156
Emerson, Ralph Waldo, 1
emotion processing, 20, 28–29, 88–90
emotional capacities
avoiding emotions, 82
coping with anxiety, 90–93
development of, 82
emotional regulation, 86–90
as essential inner resource, 17
exercise, 96–98
influences on, 82
Joseph's story, 93–98
ocean metaphor, 82
problematic nature of emotions, 81
reading resources, 167
recognizing and acknowledging emotions, 84
self-assessment, 96–98, 200–201
tolerating and accepting emotional experience, 84–85
emotional intelligence, 81, 117
emotional maturity, 102
emotional regulation
exercise, 97–98
modifying thinking, 86–87
self-assessment, 201
self-soothing, 86
taking breaks, 87–88

working through and learning from emotions, 88–90
empathy
active listening, 110, 158
in AI, 161
and apologies, 113
mutual recognition, 106–107
tolerating emotional experience, 84
encouragement, 50–51
engagement, 15
envy, 38, 53
essential ingredients, 16
essential inner resources. *See also* emotional capacities; healthy coping strategies; healthy sense of self; mental capacities; relational capacities
development of, 23–24
for mental health, 16, 17–18
self-assessment, 193–206
eudaimonic happiness, 14–15, 16
executive functioning, 66–67, 72
existential needs, 23
expectations, parental, 37
experience, new, 149–150
experiences shaping self, 187–192

F

false self, 49–50
fear
in children, 67
effect on relationships, 103
as form of motivation, 35–36
and inner dialogue, 55
investigating, 91–92
and limbic system, 71
fight, fawn, or freeze response, 90
flourishing, 12–13, 170
focus
on behavior, 109
challenge of, 72–73
exercise, 78
mindfulness and meditation, 73
self-assessment, 199
shifting, 95
Frankl, Victor, 136
Freud, Sigmund, 89
friends, 158–159
fulfillment
compared to happiness, 14–16
defined, 13–14
reading resources, 170

G

gift-giving, 173
Goleman, Daniel, 81
good judgment, 71–72, 79, 199
good mental health. *See also* personal growth
in adults, 12–13
defining, 9–11
lifelong process of maintaining, 162–164
and ongoing development, 31–32
good relationships, 15
gratitude, 53, 159
grief and loss
acceptance of, 133–134
coping capabilities, 139–141
and depression, 89
reading resources, 169
self-soothing, 86
shaping self, 44
unmourned, 89
growth, personal. *See* personal growth
guilt-tripping, 103

H

happiness
  and mental health, 3
  overview, 13–16
  reading resources, 170
harshness as form of motivation, 35–36
Harvard University, 99
healthy coping strategies
  author's story, 139–141
  development of, 124
  essential ingredients of, 130–139
  as essential inner resource, 17
  self-assessment of, 142–144, 204–206
  self-protective strategies, 124–130
healthy sense of self
  Alexander's story, 54
  balancing self-acceptance and change, 52–54, 64
  essential aspects of, 48–52
  as essential inner resource, 17
  parts of self to cultivate, 56–59
  reading resources, 168
  self-assessment of, 60–64, 193–197
  and self-talk, 55–56
hedonic happiness, 14–16
highs, chasing momentary, 14–15
human needs, 23, 28–30

I

idealization, 129–130
identifying strengths, 175–177
identity, 11, 49
implicit relational knowing, 100
inner resources. *See also* emotional capacities; healthy coping strategies; healthy sense of self; mental capacities; relational capacities
  development of, 23–24
  essential to mental health, 17–18
inner work, 31, 147–149
inpatient care, 155
insight
  into development, 30–31
  exercise, 77–78, 102
  mentalization, 70
  personal growth, 102, 147–149
  questions for, 69
  self-assessment, 198, 202
  and self-reflection, 68–70
interactions, negative, 114–116
Internal Family Systems (IFS), 155
internal operating system, 4, 19–22
internalization
  of developmental experiences, 24
  with help of therapist, 150
  of mental capacities, 65–66
  of relational experiences, 100
  sense of self, 33

J

jealousy, 53
Jed Foundation, 208

K

ketamine, 160

L

Lamott, Anne, 137
language of love, 172
languishing adults, 12
learning from emotions, 88–90
life coaching, 157
LifeRing, 208

listing
  active, 110
  and compassion, 51
  and effective communication, 113
  giving support through, 158–159
  to understand, 110–111
loss
  acceptance of, 133–134
  and depression, 89
  reading resources, 169
  shaping self, 44
  unmourned, 89
love
  language of, 172
  and sense of self, 44
loving kindness meditation, 164
Loving Self, 59, 64, 197

M

Mackesy, Charlie, 47
manipulation, 103–104
Maslow, Abraham, 10
mastery, sense of, 15, 49
MDMA-assisted therapies, 159–160
meaning
  as critical to fulfilling life, 16
  in healthy sense of self, 52, 64
  in life, 23, 159
  self-assessment, 197
meditation, 73, 159, 169
mental capacities
  development of, 65–68
  as essential inner resource, 17
  executive functioning, 66–67, 72
  focus and attention, 72–73
  functions of, 66
  good judgment and strategic planning, 71–72
  internalization, 65–66, 72
  Mia's story, 73–79
  observing mind (metacognition), 70–71
  prefrontal cortex, 66–67
  reading resources, 168
  self-assessment of, 77–79, 198–200
  self-reflection and insight, 68–70
mental health. *See also* personal growth
  in adults, 3, 12–13
  book as roadmap for, 5–7
  challenges and hopeful remedies, 3–5
  defining good, 9–11
  essential ingredients of, 16
  essential inner resources, 17–18
  importance of quality of, 1–3
  lifelong process of maintaining, 162–164
  link to happiness and fulfillment, 13–16
  and ongoing development, 31–32
  resources, 207–208
  resources for, 156–162
mental health apps, 157–159
mental illness, 3, 12–13
mentalization, 70
metacognition (observing mind), 70–71, 78
micromanaging, 92
Milton, John, 65
mind
  efficiency of, 20–22
  observing (metacognition), 70–71, 78
mindfulness, 73, 169
Mindfulness Based Therapy (MBT), 155
moderate mental health, 12
modifying thinking, 86–87
momentary highs, chasing, 14, 15
monitoring process, 111–113

Montgomery, L.M., 33
moral compass, 51, 63, 196
motivation, 35–36, 51, 55
mourning, 89, 134
mutual recognition, 105–107, 120–121, 202–203

N

NAMI (National Alliance on Mental Illness), 207
needs, human, 23, 28–30
negating, 103
negative interactions, 114–116
neglect, 25, 27–29, 124, 146
neural pathways, 21–22
neurofeedback, 156
neuroplasticity, 22
new experiences, 31, 149–150
Nin, Anaïs, 145

O

observing mind (metacognition)
  overview, 70–71
  self-assessment, 78, 198–199
obsessive-compulsive tendencies, 127
omnipotence, 127–128
organizing, 199–200
overachievers, 37

P

parts of self, 40–43
peer influence on sense of self, 38–40, 43
personal growth. *See also* development
  advocating for self, 104–105
  alternative resources for, 156–162
  and awareness, 101–105
  challenges related to, 145–147
  emotional maturity, 102
  exercise, 120
  general discussion, 162–164
  help for, 150–152
  and insight, 102, 147–149
  and new experiences, 149–150
  self-awareness, 101–102, 104
  and therapy types, 152–155
  and treatment types, 156
personal needs, 23
physical touch, 173
physiological needs, 23
planning, 199–200
podcasts, 157
positive emotions, 15
positive interactions, 114–116
positive qualities, identifying, 175–177
prefrontal cortex, 66–67
preventative care, 13
procedural knowledge, 100
procedural memory, 20
procrastination, 126
projection, 129
psilocybin-assisted therapies, 159
psychedelic-assisted therapies, 159–160
psychoanalysis, 155
Psychodynamic Diagnostic Manual (PDM-2), 10–11
psychodynamic psychotherapy, 153–154
psychotropic medications, 156
purpose, 16, 52, 64, 197

Q

quality time, 173
quick fixes, 4–5

R

rationalization, 42, 128, 130
reactivity, 25, 70–71
reading resources, 167–170
recognizing emotions, 84, 96
redirecting self-talk, 55, 56
referrals to therapists, 152
reflection
  developing capacity for, 24
  as mental capacity, 66–68
  and personal growth, 148
  self-reflection, 68–70, 77–78
regulating emotions, 201
relational capacities
  defined, 100–101
  development of, 99–100
  effective communication, 107–114
  as essential inner resource, 17
  impact of positive and negative interactions, 114–116
  internalization, 100
  Jordan and Alma's story, 116–119
  mutual recognition, 105–107
  personal growth and awareness, 101–105
  self-assessment of, 119–122, 202–204
  spectrum of, 99
relational knowing, implicit, 100
relational needs, 23
relationships
  as critical to fulfilling life, 15
  in good mental health, 11
  as mental health resource, 158–159
  reading resources, 169
  with yourself, 55–56
religions, 159
repairing ruptures, 112–113
repetition compulsion, 89
repression, 126
resilience, 167
resources, reading, 167–170
Rogers, Carl, 10
Roosevelt, Eleanor, 9

S

SAMHSA's National Helpline, 208
self-acceptance
  and change, 52–54, 64
  and happiness, 49
self-assessment
  of coping strategies, 142–144, 204–206
  of emotional capacities, 96–98, 200–201
  of healthy sense of self, 60–64, 193–197
  of mental capacities, 77–79, 198–200
  of relational capacities, 119–122, 202–204
self-awareness
  advocating for yourself, 104
  awareness of unhelpful strategies, 104
  exercise, 142
  in good mental health, 11
  healthy coping, 132–133, 138
  in healthy sense of self, 48, 60
  and personal growth and development, 101–102, 147–149
  questions for, 187–192
  self-assessment, 193–194, 204
self-care, 134–135, 143, 205
self-compassion. *See also* compassion
  in Internal Family Systems, 155
  overview, 51–52
  reading resources, 168
  self-assessment, 63, 205
self-direction, 11

self-esteem
Mia's story, 75
overview, 49
self-assessment, 61, 194–195
and social media, 38–39
self-protective strategies (defense mechanisms)
avoidance strategies, 125–126
control tactics, 126–128
denial, 128–129
extreme and aggressive measures, 129–130
overview, 124–125
self-reflection
overview, 68–70
self-assessment, 77–78, 198
self-soothing, 86
self-states, 40–43, 56–59
self-talk, 55–56, 136, 138
self-worth, 37, 49
Seligman, Martin, 15–16
sense of self. *See also* healthy sense of self
Alexander's story, 42
defined, 33
evolution of, 47
exercise, 43–45
influence of caregivers on, 34–37
influence of social environment on, 38–40
Marcus's story, 35–36
Marie's story, 37
parts of, 40–43, 56–59
questions to understand, 187–192
Sophia's story, 35, 41–42
serenity prayer, 134
service, acts of, 172
Siegel, Dan, 19
SMART Recovery, 208
social environment, 38–40, 43
social media, 38–39, 50
soothing self, 86
spirituality, 23, 159
splitting (self-protection), 128–129
spur-of-the-moment mental health resources, 157–158
stonewalling, 103
strategic planning
overview, 71–72
self-assessment, 79, 199–200
strength, tapping into, 58, 87
strengths, identifying, 175–177
Suicide and Crisis Lifeline, 207
support, giving, 158–159

T

taking breaks, 87–88
texting support, 157–159
therapy
chatbots as adjunct to, 161
and healthy sense of self, 52
and personal growth and development, 147, 150–152
types of, 152–156
thought patterns in cognitive behavioral therapy, 154
threatening, 103
3 basic steps for effective communication, 108–110, 113
time, quality, 173
tolerating emotional experience, 84–85, 97
touch, physical, 173
transcendent needs, 23
transcranial magnetic stimulation (TMS), 156

transformation, 5–6, 53, 149
trauma
  childhood, 25–26, 27–29
  effect on coping strategy development, 124
  reading resources, 170
  and sense of self, 54
Trevor Project Hotline, 207

U

unconscious mind, 20–21
unconscious processes, 153
unhelpful strategies, 103–104
unmourned losses, 89
U.S. Surgeon General, 10

V

values
  clarification exercise, 179–186
  in healthy sense of self, 51, 63
  self-assessment, 196
  and sense of self, 45
venting, 111–112

W

Waldinger, Robert, 99
Warrior Self
  healthy coping, 135, 138
  overview, 58
  self-assessment, 64, 197
ways of being, 43–45, 187–192
wellness retreats, 157
wisdom, 56–58, 59
Wise Self
  healthy coping, 138
  modifying thinking, 87
  overview, 57–58
  self-assessment, 64, 197
withdrawal, apathetic, 126
working memory, 20
working through emotions, 88–90

Author photo by Annie Barnett Photography

About the Author

Dr. Celeste Birkhofer is a licensed clinical psychologist and adjunct clinical faculty member at Stanford Medical School, Department of Psychiatry and Behavioral Sciences. She maintains a private psychotherapy practice, teaches and supervises Stanford psychiatry residents, and is on the clinical advisory board for the JED Foundation—a nonprofit dedicated to promoting emotional well-being in teens and young adults and reducing suicide risk. Her holistic approach to patient care integrates extensive experience and training in contemporary psychoanalytic and psychodynamic therapies, grief counseling, couples therapy, dialectic behavior therapy, and mindfulness and self-compassion practices.

For more information, visit Dr. Birkhofer's website: www.drcelestebirkhofer.com.